Beyond Strategy

Why is it that some companies turn out to be more successful when doing the opposite of what is prescribed in many of the current books on management and strategy?

Interestingly, many of the companies depicted as very successful companies in the standard literature end up not faring well over time—probably because they somehow end up in a dangerous autopilot mode. What this suggests is that the conventional literature isn't telling us the whole story. Even if companies have temporarily developed from an ugly duckling to a white swan, the popular recipes for success may be clipping such companies' wings.

Conversely, companies adhering to disruptive business models are seen to be more agile and to possess a higher degree of actionability. Such next generation companies are labeled black swans. They thrive because they are bold and embrace the great unknowns of tomorrow with open minds and eyes. At the same time, they are able to take advantage of incumbents' fears, risk-aversion, and blindness to what's coming. *Beyond Strategy* delves into the inner workings of such black swans as Apple, Aravind, Emirates, Huawei, Natura, Ryanair, and Tata and addresses the rise and fall of Nokia. The authors provide explosive evidence of black swan companies working against the norms to enter unchartered waters, determined not to adhere to the best practice of others, but rather to create a genuine next generation practice.

Next generation companies and their underlying philosophies are here to stay—are you?

Both authors work coherently within the space of *ABC—Academia, Business,* and Consulting.

Michael Moesgaard Andersen is an adjunct professor of strategy at Copenhagen Business School, Denmark. He runs his own venture capital company, focused on creating next generation practices. Prior to this, he was the co-owner and CEO of a medium-sized, globally focused consulting business.

Flemming Poulfelt is professor of management and strategy and vice dean at Copenhagen Business School, Denmark. He has also served on faculties at universities in Europe, the US, and Australia.

The co-authors of this book also wrote the successful title *Return on Strategy*, published by Routledge in 2010.

Beyond Strategy

The Impact of Next Generation Companies

Michael Moesgaard Andersen and Flemming Poulfelt

Routledge
Taylor & Francis Group

NEW YORK AND LONDON

First published 2014
by Routledge
711 Third Avenue, New York, NY 10017

and by Routledge
2 Park Square, Milton Park, Abingdon, Oxon OX14 4RN

Routledge is an imprint of the Taylor & Francis Group, an informa business

© 2014 Taylor & Francis

Library of Congress Cataloging-in-Publication Data
Andersen, Michael Moesgaard.
   Beyond strategy : the impact of next generation companies / Michael Moesgaard Andersen & Flemming Poulfelt. — 1 Edition.
      pages cm
   Includes bibliographical references and index.
 1. Business enterprises.   2. Strategic planning.   3. Management.   I. Poulfelt, Flemming.   II. Title.
   HF1008.A5293 2014
   658.4′012—dc23
   2013040327

ISBN: 978-0-415-53712-4 (hbk)
ISBN: 978-0-415-53713-1 (pbk)
ISBN: 978-1-315-81896-2 (ebk)

Typeset in Berling
by Apex CoVantage, LLC

Printed and bound in the United States of America by Publishers Graphics,
LLC on sustainably sourced paper.

Brief Table of Contents

Detailed Table of Contents

Foreword

For some years now we have been dealing with strategy issues from an ABC perspective—in *a*cademic research, in *b*usiness execution, and as *c*onsultants. Yet, when we look at the literature and practice, the gap between research and theory on one side and business practice on the other has widened considerably over recent years. This led us to raise a fundamental question:

> How is it that a growing number of companies are enjoying huge success despite doing the opposite of what is advised in the literature on management and strategy?

Examples are springing up at an accelerating rate too. The world's largest international airline basing itself in a desert with hardly any inhabitants let alone much business. Another toying with free flights and inviting negative publicity as a means of free marketing. A computer company achieving unprecedented levels of innovation and market disruption by deliberately building organizational silos. An eye-care specialist performing millions of surgeries for free without government subsidies. Companies instructing staff to behave as packs of wolves. An emerging-market business turning around bankrupt iconic brands from the developed West into huge profitability by applying models more usually geared to developing countries. Another emerging-market business taking on and winning in the highly competitive beauty industry with unprecedented cost structures and a reverse angle on 'beauty.'

Some of these companies' identities may be immediately identifiable. Others will come as a surprise. All will be explored in detail throughout this book.

It seems counterintuitive that companies turn out to be more successful when doing the *opposite* of what is prescribed in conventional theory. What it suggests is that conventional strategy isn't telling us the whole story, or that it may be clipping companies' wings.

With this in mind, we set out on a journey to help close the gap between theory (A) and practice (B and C), seeking both to identify defects of the conventional paradigm and to propose an emerging new paradigm—one that might better equip us to understand and explain these high-profile exceptions to the standard theory and practice. As we soon found, this means going *beyond* strategy as it is understood today.

Our first objective was to examine a number of non-conformist companies in depth, to try to establish common patterns—common traits and behaviors which might explain their degree of success given that each appears to have delivered this *as a result of* tearing up the recipes of the conventional cookbook. If we tried to analyze these businesses in the context of traditional strategy thinking, each would appear as an outlier—a blip on an otherwise pretty chart. Our view is very different—we have chosen to focus on these differences, because we believe it is what makes these companies special—and as successful as they are. To this end we have changed the terminology, preferring to think of such organizations as 'black swans' rather than outliers. An outlier is in some cases defined as companies gaining traction with an annual growth of 5%.[1] Our black swans (we will explain the metaphor in Chapter 1) are more exciting than that. They are beautiful, different, rebellious—and their presence makes an enormous splash, leaving complacent onlookers and rivals rocked by the turbulence they create.

Our work in trying to close the gap between conventional thinking on strategy, and a new emerging school of thought, has not been easy. Like the black swans we have studied, we have broken with traditional thinking. But we have had to tread carefully. To label past and present thinkers as 'old school' is to dismiss the good work that has been done on strategy to this point. Our approach is to look for what may have been missing in these approaches, and to look towards an emerging paradigm which allows for other drivers of success. Rather than talking about failed theories we have given them credit for giving rise to many attractive *white* swans—companies that developed successfully enough in their time by fulfilling their destiny as plotted by the textbooks.

We owe a huge debt of thanks to everyone who helped us in this sometimes arduous pursuit. From the academic world our heartfelt thanks go to the many reviewers who provided valuable comments to the crafting of the book. Moreover, discussions with our colleagues within Strategic Management Society and CBS were extremely helpful and beneficial. In addition we want to thank Professor Rickie Moore, EM Lyon, and Professor Kurt Motamedi, Pepperdine University, for their valuable comments in the early stages of the project.

Christina Berg Johansen, Ph.D., and now Assistant Professor undertook research responsibilities in 2012, in particular regarding a literature review of books and articles on disruption and regarding some of the black swan case companies. Sue Tabbitt did a great editing job and, like Helle Moesgaard Andersen, applied an eagle eye in polishing the final manuscript. We also owe thanks to Jette Sørensen who diligently orchestrated the administrative and secretarial tasks for us.

Special thanks go to the publisher John Szilagyi and Sharon Golan at Routledge. During John's tenure we had very constructive support in the endeavor of transforming our ideas and experiences into a book, and peer reviews from twelve professors from the wider professional academia within management and strategy. Moreover, we thank Sharon Golan for taking charge of the final stretch and for initiating the marketing of the book and the ideas behind it.

Other special thanks go to our families as they have constantly provided us with a lot of support and encouragement throughout. Without their acceptance of the many days and hours spent behind the desk and the computer the project would never have been finalized.

We also offer many thanks to business individuals with whom we have had stimulating interviews and conversations. Some also volunteered to help test and refine the metrics reproduced in Appendix 1 and 2 respectively.

Finally, we are grateful to the black swan companies whose numbers are multiplying all the time. In a world of constant change, black swans possess an unprecedented agility to adapt to new surroundings. They thrive because they are bold and embrace the great unknowns of tomorrow with outstretched wings. At the same time, they are able to take advantage of competitors' fears, risk-aversion, and blindness to what's coming.

By highlighting what these companies do differently, how and why, we hope we have uncovered something that will make for interesting reading for researchers, businesspeople, and consultants alike. Or to put it differently—for everyone who wishes to gain a greater awareness of and appreciation for the as yet great unknown; for everyone open to moving *beyond* strategy.

Michael Moesgaard Andersen and Flemming Poulfelt

Copenhagen, April 29, 2014

NOTE

1 McGrath, Rita Gunther (2013), *The End of Competitive Advantage*, Harvard Business Press, Boston, see p. 15f, where an outlier is defined as a publicly traded company with a market capitalization of over USD 1 billion at the end of 2009, having grown revenue or net income by at least 5% every year for the preceding five years. None of our 'black swans' appear in the part of the sample which she outlines, as our black swans do not meet her criteria. One of several differences is that most of our black swans are not publicly traded companies—maybe therefore better able to take the market by surprise?! See also Sydney Finkelstein et al. (2007), *Breakout Strategy: Meeting the challenge of double-digit growth*, McGraw Hill, New York, where other than stock-listed companies are included in the sample, and where the focus on put on double-digit growth.

Introduction
Can You Predict the Unexpected?

The famous fairytale author H.C. Andersen wrote in *The Ugly Duckling:*[1]

> Then he felt quite ashamed, and hid his head under his wing; for he did not know what to do, he was so happy, and yet not at all proud. He had been persecuted and despised for his ugliness, and now he heard them say he was the most beautiful of all the birds.

How often is this same philosophy applied to business strategy—the idea that a company can only fulfill its true potential once it goes through a predestined process and achieves the accepted embodiment of beauty and success?

Conventional strategy is so often about crafting a quick and sustainable fix based on known best practices—one that expeditiously converts the ugly duckling into a white swan. It is about conducting diligent and rational work to create an entity (a 'white swan' company) that conforms to known criteria, giving it the best chance of achievement. But is this really the best path to success, especially in today's dynamic business environment?

The renowned philosopher Karl Popper once advised that researchers should look not only for the obvious. Continuing with the swan metaphor, it is generally observed (certainly in the Western hemisphere) that such birds are white. On the basis of this experience, many people would confidently conclude that there are only white swans, forming a common body of knowledge that is accepted by the majority.

The human mind is geared towards dealing with phenomena and things we know we know. Once we 'know' something, this determines what we see. If we believe that there are only white swans, we tend to affirm this knowledge by only looking for and mentally registering white swans. We do not consider the possibility that there may also be black swans, for example. They are outside our experience and therefore our mindset, so we do not seek them out. If or when black swans enter our consciousness, perhaps because we catch a glimpse of one when travelling abroad, our reaction is one of surprise—causing us to question our previously held assumptions.

We have drawn on this white/black swan metaphor in our research into business strategy, and the way that companies act strategically, which will be discussed in this book. Our contention is that conventional strategy, which aims to create 'white swan companies' (those that follow known models) rather than 'black swan companies' (which buck the trend), needs to be challenged.

The mainstream of existing literature on strategy focuses predominantly on the white swan, or the accepted contributors to success, so we will present our own research within this context. But, more importantly, we will expand on our research into *black* swan companies, and discuss its relevance today—in the context of an emerging 'new strategy' paradigm and the need for *new* principles, models, and tools, so that companies are presented with means of measurement for successful transformation.

Our instinct as human beings is primarily towards rational planning. We are programmed to think that if we work diligently, performing thorough analyses, conducting a phased and well-structured strategy program, and basing our activities on best practice and existing knowledge, we are maximizing our chances of success. Within the field of management and strategy, we can see the evidence of this 'recipe for success' approach—in that the overwhelming majority of existing literature resembles a cookbook with specific ingredients and steps to follow.

Yet these formulae don't—and can't—guarantee long-term success, because they do not cater for the unknown.

Our research suggests that, while 'proven' recipes may have helped some companies achieve some degree of success in the past and in the present, they are less effective in ensuring sustained long-term performance—as can be seen when companies are tracked over a longer time frame. In keeping with this, while conventional strategy literature is able to retrospectively address why some companies have emerged as a success (i.e. as white swans), it has been less useful in determining why some of these businesses—which once looked so strong and healthy—have later lost their sheen.

Why is it that many white swans regress, digress, or disappear having followed a 'good' recipe? And how come others—the black swans, which have not followed tried-and-tested business approaches—have managed to achieve a very high return on their strategy?

The 'cookbook' strategy literature does not provide a satisfactory answer to such questions. The phenomenon is comprehensively documented in our book, *Return on Strategy*™. There we highlighted findings of the potential for a *higher* Return on Strategy if companies do not adhere to prescribed (recipe-for-success) strategies, but instead leave room for the X factor—'the unknown' or 'the unexpected.'

Interestingly, many of the companies depicted as very successful companies in the cookbook literature end up not faring well over time—probably because they are blindly following a formula based on past success. This puts many companies in a dangerous autopilot mode; they become arrogant and complacent, and they lose their edge, which is essential to competitiveness. Conversely, companies that do not conform and which remain open to new models are seen to be more agile, and to possess a higher degree of responsiveness, than companies confined to a rigid template.

Inspired by these findings, we have focused subsequent research on the fortunes of companies that have rejected the cookbook approach to business strategy. After analyzing a number of sample companies, we found clear 'black swan' characteristics—evidence that these companies break the mold. In our eagerness to learn more about what these companies do differently, we asked them a couple of questions, to determine:

- What characterizes black swans and what differentiates them from white swans and other companies?
- Whether existing literature on management and strategy is able to predict the emergence of black swans?

Generally, our research has shown that there is a considerable amount of 'reverse thinking' present in and around black swan companies. Prevailing strategies indicate that such companies tend to subscribe to disruptive strategies and act radically differently, with a very short time to market.

Numerous other characteristics can be attached to black swan companies and our research shows that the conventional paradigm is generally insufficient to deal with such companies. Rather, we are watching a new paradigm emerge based on various types of disruption, unprecedented thinking that outperforms conventional rational behavior, and deliberate ways to distort market mechanisms.

In short, black swans deliver the unexpected with disruptive implications.

Both management and research are far too often focused on rigorous explanations of the homogeneous, while overlooking extreme heterogeneity, such as outliers. Generally, black swans are outliers. In most cases outliers are dismissed from research where focus has been on the homogeneous average and regression to the mean. Outliers have therefore been disregarded in order "to keep the graph nicely scaled", or to "counter the bias introduced by potential outliers," as described in research.[2]

Naturally, taking outliers into account implicates a development towards increased heterogeneity and therefore an increase in uncertainty and risk. This prompts a related question: *Can you predict the unexpected?*

Already, from the outset of this book, a partial answer may be provided: if you are working only within the framework of conventional theory and thinking, you will be unable to predict or plan for the unexpected.

A closer look at one of the definitions of an outlier may be helpful in this context:

> An observation which deviates so much from other observations as to arouse suspicion that it was generated by a different mechanism.[3]

This 'different mechanism' is particularly interesting. As black swans generally do not buy into the recipes of the conventional paradigm, the search for this mechanism invariably leads us to something that is in contrast to the conventional paradigm.

Although the aspiration to fully discover this 'different mechanism' is strong, realistically the scope and ambition of this book is mainly to address the inner workings of black swan companies. Specifically we will be seeking to determine how this relates to both the conventional paradigm (focus on finding a simple recipe for success) and the emerging new paradigm (paying attention to the unknown universe, being disruptive by nature, exercising reverse thinking, preparing for the unplanned, and using capabilities ambidextrously).

By gaining a better understanding of black swan companies and the emerging new paradigm, it is our hope that the reader will arrive at a richer insight into the largely unknown and little understood world of extreme outliers. We hope this journey will be of equal interest to you irrespective of whether your aim is to co-create a black swan business; to prepare yourself against the hugely disruptive effect of these less familiar entities; or to teach or study the emergence of a new paradigm as a professor, MBA student, management consultant, investment banker, or stock broker.

Supposition: If we are able to adjust our mindset towards the emerging paradigm, new doors will open to us.

This way we are now confirming the journey commenced by the title *Return on Strategy*[TM] as it is possible to achieve a higher Return on Strategy when moving from conventional thinking towards the ambidextrous mindset of the emerging paradigm.[4]

NOTES

1 H.C. Andersen (1844), *The Ugly Duckling* (translation).
2 These two quotes come from, respectively Fuentelsaz, L. et al. (2012), Production technologies and financial performance: The effect of uneven diffusion among competitors. *Research Policy* 41(2), 401–413; Rope, S. et al. (2008), Modelling the innovation value chain, *Research Policy*, 37(6–7),

961–977. These were also part of the presentation by Markus Paukku (Outlier organizations and systemic transitions: Towards a research agenda) at the SMS conference in 2012 in Prague.

3 From Hawkins, D.M. (1980), *Identification of Outliers,* Chapman, London.

4 See Andersen, Froholt, and Poulfelt (2010), *Return on Strategy: How to achieve it!,* Routledge, Abingdon, Oxon., UK. We have retained the trade mark protection to the notions of Return on Strategy™. See also www.returnonstrategy.org.

Part I

From the Conventional to the Emerging New Paradigm

Chapter 1

Disrupters' Paradise

IS OUR MINDSET GEARED TOWARDS A REALITY THAT DOESN'T EXIST?

> Americans have an obsession with the quick fix, and nowhere has the idea of a magic formula been more fervently embraced than in the ranks of American management.

This was the introduction to Michael E. McGill's book, *American Business and the Quick Fix*, published in 1988.[1] Having heavily criticized the existing literature on management and strategy and also the MBA schools' support for quick fixes, he concluded in the last chapter that:

> American management is in "a hell of a fix"! This simple, declarative observation describes a variety of conditions true of management and managers today. Certainly the noun sense of fix applies. Even the most naïve observer of business recognizes the awkward situation, the dilemma, the predicament of managers today (McGill, p. 201).

McGill's book did not receive much attention and is not quoted in many of the very popular American textbooks, perhaps because he was critical in his approach to the idea of a 'magic formula.' As will be expanded on in Chapter 2, the overwhelming majority of the literature within the field of management and strategy originates from the US and is, by and large, to be found within the context of the magic formula (also labeled 'the golden recipe'). This is interesting not only in an American context but also globally due to the considerable American impact on business thinking globally. It also has as much resonance today as it did when McGill's book was first issued in 1988.

The bias towards the development and application of a simple recipe, which in an intuitively rational way exhausts the actions necessary for success, has important implications. These are crucial in understanding a new type of company which typically arrives on the scene unexpectedly and with disruptive success. The emergence of so-called 'black swans' can take whole industries by surprise.

When the mindset among academics and managers is geared towards intuitively rational strategic thinking, where is the mental space for success delivered through the unexpected, through irrationalities, unforeseen tactics, the X factor, and so on? The short answer is that there *is* no room!

It is this blinkered outlook that has paved the way for the emergence of black swans, and created a kind of disrupters' paradise. It is far easier for black swans to disrupt when they are met with no response, laidback surprise, and a complacent 'watch-and-see' attitude. Black swan companies almost have a free lunch as long as our thinking is steered towards a reality that either doesn't exist or is blurred.

Conventional companies typically develop their business strategies by pairing their own knowledge with that of the external strategy adviser, and by referring to what they perceive to be solid and undisputable knowledge. However, as we shall see throughout this book, black swans operate on the basis of unknowns—i.e. by addressing what they *know* they don't know, or by anticipating the completely unknown. This ability to acknowledge, embrace, and be ready for what is not yet known gives black swans an important edge over conventional companies.

IS IT SUFFICIENT TO BE HATCHED IN A SWAN'S EGG?

Many companies fare well by starting off as ugly ducklings and then, over the decades, developing into white swans. Much of the conventional literature on management and strategy is based on the aspiration to bring companies to the white swan stage, where they fulfill the evolutionary plan and truly fly. Such companies are not in the main the focus of this book; rather, these pages are dedicated to the phenomenon of black swan companies—businesses that find their own way to successful flight, without the expected process of conventional metamorphosis.

Consider Ryanair which in the space of just a few years gained the position as the largest inter-Europe airline, carrying more than 75 million passengers, disrupting a number of established white swan carriers. A further example is the growth rates of Emirates and Etihad, airlines originating in the United Arabic Emirates; both have commanded unexpectedly sizeable market shares and have turned their home locations into preferred international flight hubs and destination cities. Then there was Apple's invention of the iPhone and its associated business model, which propelled the company to dizzy new heights while disrupting a number of white swan mobile phone manufacturers. Another example is Chinese telecommunication solution provider Huawei, which was not taken seriously by the white swans in its industry, yet quickly took the number one slot in its market.

Where Does the Black Swan Metaphor Come From?

The phenomenon of a so-called black swan is the appearance in real life of an animal or a company that nobody had expected. Most people have only seen white swans so they infer from this that only white swans exist. Similarly, no one is prepared for black swan companies.

The term black swan is borrowed from Nassim Nicholas Taleb's eponymous book. He uses the term to address the philosophical problem of "the impossibility of calculating the risks of consequential rare events and predicting their occurrence."[2] For our purposes, the term is applied at a more disaggregated level, i.e. at the company level or even at the individual level, and in conjunction with strategies which seem to be disruptive by nature.[3]

The rare and unexpected events fostered by black swan companies are the point of departure for this book. Instead of looking at averages, statistical correlations and forecasting based on past performance, we have taken as our evidence a credible number of companies that have succeeded without conforming to accepted business strategies. By taking a manageable sample of such specimens, we have been able to delve deep into the inner workings of these new types of companies. It is only by looking at the intricate behavior of individual companies, departments, innovative business units, and single personalities that we are able to observe the important micro-foundations for black swan successes.

Notable Black Swan Events

Apple's history is a long and involved affair, marked by a number of distinct phases. First was the sudden emergence of the user-friendly personal computer (Macintosh in 1984)—something that consumers did not yet know they needed. In this sense, this episode resembles a black swan event, albeit that its potential impact didn't fully materialize due to Microsoft's rapid commercialization of its own graphically controlled operating system. Despite some reasonable years, Apple's success did not live up to its early promise and the company did not fulfill its real potential until its very disruptive foray into music, smartphones, tablet computing, and digital publishing.

A closer look at the inner workings of Apple reveals a black swan transformation of the company and the emergence of a more dynamic business.

Black Swan Influencers

Looking at Apple from a historical perspective it can be argued that John Sculley, who took over in 1985 (when Steve Jobs left the company), followed a white swan strategy based on his experiences from the retail industry (he came from Pepsi). It was during this period that Apple's profile as an innovator and prominent player was arguably at its lowest. When Steve Jobs returned to Apple and later took over the CEO role, he reintroduced a fresh outlook and culture of innovation to the company. During Jobs' reign, Apple produced some revolutionary products and completely changed the way people communicate and consume content. The rest, as they say, is history.

When we turn to the micro-foundation of Huawei, it is striking to consider the personal background of founder Ren Zhengei. His military roots shaped the company's corporate mindset so that sales teams were referred to as 'market guerrillas', and market strategy in terms of 'countryside surrounding cities' and the need to "develop a pack of wolves."[4] By seeing things differently, he was able to command an authoritative position in the market.

How Are Black Swans Different?

The black swan is characterized as something completely unexpected, and something which is largely unexplainable—something which does not make sense to people who only expect to see white swans. The black swan is a true outlier. Conventional firms converge around the mathematical mean of the Bell curve based on known metrics, while the black swan often operates on the basis of metrics that are not yet known, throwing out the neat graph and challenging existing assumptions in a highly disruptive way.

As recently as just a few years ago, nobody would have expected Apple to enter the smartphone market, still less have the phenomenal success it has enjoyed with its App Store. Market leader Nokia was slow to react, and when it did launch a counterattack it was too late; as a result Nokia lost market share at a faster rate than it was able to adjust its cost structure. The upshot was a drop in share price to a tenth of the value it had held before Apple launched its assault on the then fledgling smartphone market.

Similarly, traditional airlines have seen their market and business models challenged. Just a few years ago, it would have been unthinkable to the market leaders that flights would be promoted free of charge, yet this is precisely what Ryanair and some of the other rule-breakers have begun to experiment with.

What is most striking about black swans above all is the impact they have on their environment. This is twofold. The first effect is the sheer growth of the black swan itself, and the speed at which they absorb market share from established rivals, as has been seen with Ryanair, Apple, Emirates, Etihad, Huawei, and other black swans.

Another, to some extent overlooked attribute of the black swan, is the disruptive effect they have on the wider business environment. Very often market segments converge resulting in a zero-sum game where consumers' expenditure does not exceed a certain threshold. Consequently the success of the black swan is usually in direct proportion to the strategic and financial failure of traditional market players. In short, black swans deliberately create value while simultaneously removing a relatively large proportion of value from competitors.

To summarize, the black swan is synonymous with disruption. It is not a friendly beast whose presence everyone welcomes, as could be considered to be the case with white swans—because their existence is expected and their traits well understood, meaning they can be enjoyed for what they are. The black swan, by contrast, is an often unwelcome outlier whose propensity to thrive is based on its ability to disrupt and take away from others, destroying existing incumbents which do not have the mindset or agility to respond adequately and in a timely fashion.

The black swan is *not* the ugly duckling hatched from a swan's egg and fulfilling its destiny in the expected way. Rather it may burst onto the scene, fully formed, unabashed by its different plumage, and ready to menace. It is the author of its own fairytale—one with a dark twist.

ARE WHITE SWANS REALLY DISRUPTED BY BLACK SWANS?

White swans are often characterized by a certain level of complacency. Once a company has reached the white swan stage, everyone views it as a success. As human beings we have an inbuilt preference for success. With reference to Karl Popper, we tend to use our energy to verify a success (rather than to look for falsification).

Nokia provides an example of an ugly duckling that over time grew to become a white swan. In the 1970s and 1980s the Nordic Mobile Telephone (NMT) system was rolled out in Nordic countries, and then beyond. The system was designed to be open, a relatively new principle at that time, which allowed mobile devices to be supplied by different manufacturers and for mobile telephony users to roam internationally. In order to draw Finland in as a major partner in this Nordic collaboration, Nokia was encouraged to participate in the development and manufacturing of mobile devices.

At the time Nokia made rubber boots and a number of other products not related to mobile communications, giving it the appearance of an ugly duckling. Nokia responded to the prompt gratefully, and in the 1980s set all sails to the wind to develop mobile phones. Its chance to expand geographically came in the 1990s with GSM, providing global sales opportunities in a growing market. Nokia went through several phases, repositioning the company and spring-cleaning the product portfolio—throwing out the rubber boots in favor of mobile phones and subsequently equipment for mobile networks.

Over the next twenty years Nokia managed to build up a mobile phone market share of more than 40% on the back of its first-mover experience in the Nordic market, and diligently worked to create a new ecosystem through which customers learned to use their mobile phones as a lifestyle accessory—as an alarm clock, calculator, text messenger, and camera, as well as for MMS and SMS-based downloads, and so on. Repeat purchases of Nokia devices were common too, because of the ease of recharging as there was always a Nokia recharger around. Nokia had truly emerged as a market leader.

However, with the development of smartphones and app stores, Nokia suddenly lost momentum and was knocked down by both Apple and the Android operating system. In the space of just two to three years, Nokia moved from the position as market leader in the mobile space to a marginal position. But how was it that Nokia failed to thrive in the smartphone market when it had devoted more resources than anyone else to developing the handsets? At the low end of the market Nokia lost out to Southeast Asian competitors despite being the market leader. It also surrendered its position as a leading infrastructure vendor, thereby losing the dynamic interplay between terminals and infrastructure. But what was it that caused the company to lose momentum?

The answer lies with the disruptive influence of the black swan. But how and why the white swan fell victim to its appearance is the more curious part. To explain this, we need to look at how our brains work.

WHY DO OUR BRAINS REGISTER WHITE SWANS RATHER THAN BLACK SWANS?

Nokia did not anticipate the emergence of a black swan. It perceived its competitors to be white swans players trying to feed in the usual way in the usual places. Nokia is far from alone in exhibiting these qualities. It is normal to default to the obvious, and to expect the expected. Being able to anticipate the sudden arrival of black swans when these are outside the parameters of our usual experience is very difficult to do.

We can be blind to the obvious, and we are also blind to our blindness.

This is how psychologist Daniel Kahneman has summarized this phenomenon.[5] He makes a distinction between 'fast thinking' and 'slow thinking.' In the context of management and strategy issues, it is particularly interesting that Kahneman has identified an inconsistency built into our minds. "Our minds are susceptible to systematic errors" as he puts it (p. 10), or "Our associate systems tends to settle on a coherent pattern of activation and suppress doubt and ambiguity" (p. 87f.).

A telling experiment conducted by Chabris and Simons[6] involves volunteers who were asked to watch a basketball game between two teams and to count the number of passes made by one of the sides. During the course of the game a woman dressed in a gorilla suit suddenly runs onto the court and beats her chest like a gorilla, before disappearing again. The mental effort and concentration of carrying out the programmed task meant that many of the volunteers insisted that they had not seen the gorilla or that there was no gorilla. The programmed task had blinded them. Their brains were so taken up with the required task that they were unable to register the unexpected.

We can substitute the volunteers with Nokia and the gorilla with Apple. Nokia's strategic resources were programmed to a rational continued execution of the company's agreed business strategy, in which there was no room for the unexpected gorilla success of an iPhone. Turning this situation on its head, Apple relied heavily on the blind spots of Nokia and other competitors to achieve the disruption it planned.

We will look into these mechanisms in greater detail later in the book and also consider the findings at a more generic level. The mental disposition, reactions, and non-reactions of the volunteers (and of Nokia) go some way to explaining why conventional strategy thinking—driven by a recipe game—can be dangerous, in that it focuses too heavily on the creation of white swans, leaving no mental space for black swans.

In the business world this points to one of the reasons why good companies go bad. According to Sheth[7], 'competitive myopia' can mean a company is too focused to see what may be coming left field, because they lack broader perspective. Such a company defines the competition too narrowly and suffers from a "lack of the peripheral vision that would discern less obvious challengers—those whose threat is, for whatever reason, not on today's radar screen but is nonetheless very real and dangerous" (Sheth, p. 133). Another vulnerability Sheth highlights is complacency. There are numerous examples of companies going down the drain because the top management has demonstrated complacent behavior. Some have argued that this was the case with Nokia.

Conventional thinking tends to assume that people and organizations are independent rational agents. As demonstrated in the gorilla case this is also supported by our brain activity. What is experienced as rational decision making is driven by something we are not aware of, such as a programmed instinct to follow what others do (the herd tendency); an inbuilt trust towards our own group while at the same time a hostility to outsiders; and a low capacity to remember disasters and to disregard the likelihood of reoccurrences. In short, such effects cause us to be blindsided. An onlooker might say that working so rationally and dispassionately as we conventionally do is equal to wandering around with blinkers on.

As long as we continue with this way of thinking, the way is open for black swans to enter center stage.

HOW TO RECOGNIZE A BLACK SWAN COMPANY

Broadly speaking there are five common characteristics to a black swan company or market disrupter.

1. A black swan company and market disrupter does not just represent marginal impact but implies *extreme consequences* for the business environment.
2. This impact is double-edged, representing *positive impact* (value creation and positive numbers) for the black swan and *negative impact* for other market participants affected by the disruption—for example by way of value destruction and negative growth. This doesn't have to mean a zero-sum game (Apple's App Store is an example of how a black swan can generate an ecosystem which in itself generates positive effects in sub-segments).
3. A black swan is an *outlier*, in that it is far outside the realm of regular industry expectations.
4. A black swan makes its appearance *unexpectedly*, in a way that could not have been predicted.
5. To some extent, these attributes make it almost impossible to establish or maintain a firm distinction between the crafting of the disruptive strategy and the execution. This is because some of the black swan's disruptive effects are tied to the way the strategy is executed when the surprise element is taken into account—as the disruptive strategy is very often carried out in an *accelerated* fashion, reducing or extinguishing response options.

The black swan company pursuing a disruptive strategy normally exhibits all five of these attributes. It demonstrates not incremental, evolutionary conduct but rather a conscious attack on existing businesses with a revolutionary effect.[8] Thus, disruptive strategy thinking implies conflicts and aggression. Value is not created in a harmonious world where there is a win-win for everyone. The disruptive strategy only generates value if disruption also takes place.

In a multipolar world, affected by cyclical financial crises, increasing tensions due to population issues, religion, scarcity, or perceived scarcity of resource, it is time for business leaders, management consultants, MBA students, investment bankers, and board members to reconsider whether it is justifiable and defensible to continue adhering to the belief that we are in a harmonious win-win universe. It is more reasonable to assume that we are acting within a universe which is increasingly tainted by a conflict-based, zero-sum game where substantial value can only be created in one part of the chain by destroying value in another part.

Our goal is to explore these black swan attributes in more detail than has previously been attempted in strategy literature.

IBM undertook a study some years ago on how CEOs from all over the world perceived the 'enterprise of the future.'[9] Among the proposed characteristics were that the enterprise of the future would be 'disruptive by nature,' meaning that they would be able to outperform and pursue even more disruptive business model innovations than their underperforming peers. In keeping with similar studies, the exercise showed that today's and tomorrow's high achievers are making major business model changes more frequently, and are more likely to pursue industry model innovation, than more conventional players.

According to IBM, the enterprise of the future continually searches for new ways to compete. Common attributes proposed by the study are that such an enterprise:

- thinks like an outsider;
- draws breakthrough ideas from other industries;
- empowers entrepreneurs;
- experiments creatively in the market, not just the lab; and
- manages today's business while experimenting with tomorrow's model.

The point here is that disruptive behavior and efforts are what it will take to truly differentiate the business of tomorrow.

In this book we will explore how black swan companies operate and see how their disruptive strategies are not only tied to innovation and technology, but to all of the design parameters of a strategy geared towards achieving a high return. Key success drivers may include revising the product portfolio, leveraging the financial circuit, optimizing the organizational design, exploiting customer attitudes, and fostering leadership genes. In short, when we talk about black swans and their disruptive potential, we are really talking about the comprehensive corporate strategy of such a company.

A VIEW FROM THE HILLTOP

Is it possible to predict the unexpected?

This is a question which is addressed in the following chapters. In Chapter 2, we will look into current management thinking and subsequent strategy practice. A key point made in this chapter is the observation that much of the conventional thinking within management and strategy emanates from the US. Somewhat surprisingly, a number of the recipes from the cookbook literature fail to pass the litmus test in helping to shed light on disruptive companies. One of the reasons for this is that this literature only deals with the known universe and indeed only selected parts of this universe—typically reduced to past performance of stock-listed American companies. Intricate uncertainties from the (yet) unknown universe are not addressed at all. In leaving this gap, such tomes push open the door for the emergence of black swan companies, leaving white swan companies almost defenseless—allowing more Apples to sneak up on Nokias, and more would-be Southwest Airlines to take share from United Airlines equivalents.

Chapter 3 begins by exploring the notion of disruption in more detail—what is disruption, how has the concept been dealt with in existing literature, and how does it relate to the emerging new paradigm? Dealing with such questions brings us on to the importance of mindset, its role in disruption, and in the emerging paradigm.

Chapter 4 offers a more detailed look at the emerging paradigm. We introduce a number of traits that are not fully developed in the existing literature but which are highly relevant in our understanding of black swan companies. The chapter ends by looking at the terminology of the conventional paradigm versus that of the emerging new paradigm. In this way we are able to illustrate how the emerging paradigm shift is being accelerated by the emergence of black swans, and how it will continue to gather momentum in a tsunami-like fashion. Chapter 4 concludes Part I of the book.

Part II (Chapters 5–12) addressees the inner workings of black swan companies. Here we take a closer look at examples including Apple, Aravind, Emirates, Huawei, Natura, Nokia, Ryanair, and Tata. Each case is different (it is the conventional paradigm which implies all successful companies are or need to be similar), but we analyze the black swan traits shown by each company, recognizing that these may be manifested in a different form and style from one case to another.

Part III (Chapter 13 and Appendices 1 and 2) of the book offers our conclusions, a deeper dive into the emerging paradigm, and further food for thought. Chapter 13 will recapitulate the lessons learned from the inner workings of black swan companies and their micro-foundations. In this way we seek to give the reader some answers to the question posed earlier—i.e. whether the unpredictable can be predicted.

The Appendices present useful metrics and a wider toolkit for companies that want to improve the stewardship of top management in these more turbulent times where unpredictability is on the increase.

Our goal is that this book will be relevant both for those looking to craft and optimize a black swan strategy, and for conventional companies wishing to avoid being disrupted by a black swan. We hope our discussions will also appeal to onlookers interested in gaining a clearer understanding of why white swans appear to face bigger and bigger problems every day, whether they are stock-brokers, investment bankers, or others within the broader financial sector.

Part I, then, focuses on the shift from a conventional paradigm to an emerging new paradigm. This part of the book is largely theoretical. Part II addresses the inner workings of selected black swan companies. This part is largely empirical. Part III offers our final analysis, an outlook, and an exclusive toolbox, so that companies can boost the return on their future strategy. This part of the book is designed to be practical, if not operational.

KEY REFLECTIONS

A. The purpose of this book is to address the growing gap between the highly popular cookbook literature and the increasing number of black swan companies which do not fit into the existing theories. We argue that this calls for a paradigm shift within strategic theories and concepts.

B. Conventional strategy is very much about an *evolutionary* path, bringing companies from the ugly duckling stage to the white swan stage. However, we see an increasing number of companies develop very quickly and quash their peers. We ask: have we underestimated the role and impact of black swan companies?

C. Within the field of strategy much attention is drawn to existing knowledge, things that we know we know, so that we can plan our strategy diligently and rationally. However, almost all disruption comes as a surprise for existing companies. Here we explore whether we are blind to our own blindness. Can we continue to work only with the 'knowns' in strategy, while disregarding the 'unknowns'?

NOTES

1 McGill, Michael E. (1988), *American Business and the Quick Fix*, Henry Holt, New York.

2 Taleb, Nassim Nicholas (2010), *The Black Swan: The impact of the highly improbable*, Random House, New York.

3 The term 'black swan' is also being used by consultants in other contexts than originally sought by Taleb, see e.g. *The Future of Telecoms: New models for a new industry*, 2012 by Delta Partners. They address 'market black swans' (e.g. p. 10). We now take this one step further and create a closer link between 'black swan' and company strategy and management.

4 See the deeper analysis in Andersen, Froholt, and Poulfelt (2010) *Return on Strategy*, e.g. ch. 9, pp. 164ff.

5 Kahneman, Daniel (2011), *Thinking, Fast and Slow*, Allen Lane, London.

6 Chabris, Christopher and Simons, Daniel (2011), *The Invisible Gorilla and Other Ways Our Intuition Deceives Us*, HarperCollins, London.

7 Sheth, Jagdish (2007), *The Self-Destructive Habits of Good Companies*, Wharton School Publishing, Upper Saddle River, NJ.

8 We tend not to use Kuhn's notion of paradigm shift at this stage, primarily because his terminology has been widely overused and misused. Essentially, we are depicting and describing an emerging paradigm in Kuhn's original meaning of a paradigm shift, as we are moving from the conventional paradigm assuming strict rationalism to an emerging new paradigm characterized by intuition, seemingly irrationality, turning upside down, etc.

9 IBM Global CEO Study (2008), *The Enterprise of the Future.*

Chapter 2

The Conventional Paradigm

HOW BUSINESSES BECOME BLIND

Having already set out a number of examples of and reasons for the so-called disrupters' paradise, we aim in this chapter to investigate just one of them, namely old-school thinking—based on existing management and strategy literature. This is known as the conventional paradigm, often constituting a common body of knowledge about what is right or wrong when managing and developing strategies for companies. This accepted knowledge pool became so credible that MBAs, managers, executives, board directors, consultants, and many others have followed the 'rules' blindly for decades.

THE OLD SCHOOL

The following observations provide an overview of conventional thinking within strategic management. 'Conventional' can be interpreted to mean 'traditional with inherent defects' or to put it more bluntly 'American old-school thinking.' This contrasts with the emerging new paradigm of which reverse-thinking is a major component.

In order to comprehensively characterize the conventional paradigm, we need to take a closer look at the existing literature which traditionally has been very American in its bias. The bestselling books on successful business strategies and strategic management were first published in the US, and based largely on American (typically stock-listed) companies, and it was these that were used in teaching programs at MBA schools. As a result of this application, some of the literature is MBA centric; this in turn created a strong tailwind, as cookbooks taught at MBA schools went on to be used extensively by top-level managers and consultants following graduation.[1]

RECIPES FOR GOOD (OR BAD?) STRATEGIC MANAGEMENT!

The bestselling books fall into two broad categories. One category is made up of so-called recipe literature[2] in the wider context of strategic management. Another category comprises literature which is less (if at all) focused on management, and comparatively more focused on strategy—notably corporate strategy.

Examples of the former can be seen in Table 2.1, divided under four 'recipe' book types.

Table 2.1
The Four Recipes on Strategic Management Compared

In Search of Excellence	Built to Last	Good to Great	What Really Works
A bias for action	Big Hairy Audacious Goals	Level 5 Leadership	Clear strategy
Close to the customer	Cult-like cultures	First Who, Then What	Focus on execution
Autonomy and entrepreneurship	Try a Lot of Stuff and Keep What Works	Confront the Brutal Facts	Culture of high performance
Productivity through people	Home-grown Management	The Hedgehog Concept	Structured to reduce bureaucracy
Hands-on, value driven	Good Enough Never Is	Culture of Discipline	Talent must be hired, developed, and retained
Stick to the knitting		Technology Accelerators	Innovative products and services anticipating disruptive events
Simple form, lean staff			Leadership through great chief executives
Simultaneous loose-tight properties			Mergers and partnerships as a vehicle for high performance

STICKING TO THE RECIPE

Managerial recipes are beliefs and approaches based on experiences that have been developed over time until they have become institutionalized. When a business formula has worked once, it is often convenient to believe that it will do so again.

Since the 1980s much of the management literature has been characterized by its attempts to identify and describe the recipe for success. Success is often defined as something equal to superior performance, measured by growth in stock price and actual profitability numbers. Despite providing valuable insight, none of the recipes offered over the past three decades have stood the test of time in the changing world of business and strategy.

EXCELLENCE IS IN THE EYE OF THE BEHOLDER

In 1977 two McKinsey consultants, Tom Peters and Robert H. Waterman, were put in charge of a project concerning organizational effectiveness. This project led to the publication of what is arguably the first bestselling book on management and how to become successful. First published in 1982 the book, *In Search of Excellence: Lessons from America's Best-Run Companies*, became an instant hit with business leaders in America who were desperately seeking a winning formula in the face of growing competition from Asian companies in particular, and the economic downturn of the 1980s.

The findings of the book were based on a sample group of 62 American companies of which 43 were labeled as excellent. Entry into the club of excellence was awarded according to three quantitative measures for growth, three quantitative measures for return on capital, and finally a qualitative measure for the capacity to innovate.[3]

Having identified the 43 best and most innovative companies, the authors continued to search for common attributes that could then be argued to constitute the building blocks of excellence. They identified eight attributes of corporate excellence which are listed in Table 2.1.

Selling more than three million copies in the first four years alone, the book became a long-lasting success not only in the US but also globally. The success of the book however was not mirrored in all of the 43 companies it identified as being excellent performers. In 1984, only two years after publication, the book was reviewed in a *Business Week* article "Oops. Who's Excellent Now?"[4] This revealed that around one third of the 43 companies were now experiencing financial difficulties. Among the less fortunate companies listed as excellent performers in the Peters and Waterman bestseller are Atari, Digital Equipment Corporation (DEC), and Wang Laboratories, of which none exist today.

In contrast, companies such as Exxon, General Electric, Ingersoll-Rand, and United Technologies that did not gain entry to the club of excellence are still in existence today.

In the case of Atari, the fall from excellence is believed to result from the company's failure to develop and market products to succeed the hugely popular Atari 2600 video game console, and to capitalize on the emergence of the home computer. What is known as the North American video game crash of 1983 also piled additional problems onto a troubled Atari and the share price of Warner, its owner, tumbled from USD 60 to 20.[5] In 1984 Warner sold off the home computing and games console division to Jack Tremiel for USD 240 million. Under this new leadership the business continued to develop state-of-the-art consoles, but failed to market these with any significant success, thus losing market share to Nintendo's Game Boy. The failure to market its products, and the desire of the Tremiel family to exit the business, eventually led to the demise of Atari.

DEC's undoing is quite remarkable considering that the company was among the largest computer manufacturers in the world by the late 1980s, and considered by many to have been the creator of the minicomputer and arguably the first computers for personal use. At its peak DEC employed some 100,000 people with subsidiaries across the globe, but a desire to branch out into other complementary disciplines such as software, as well as a strong aversion to traditional marketing, in tandem with the rise of RISC-based architecture, ultimately led to the demise of the company.

Wang Labs was founded by Dr. An Wang and Dr. G.Y. Chu in 1951, and manufactured calculators, word processors, and personal computers. At the height of the business in the 1980s the company had annual revenues in the region of USD 3 billion and employed around 40,000 people. It is a common belief that Wang's subsequent failure stemmed from a narrow focus on computers designed specifically for word processing, and a lack of industrial foresight, as general computers would take the place of computers designed for a single purpose only.

So what was the cause of these three companies' undoing? Did they stray from the recipe laid out by Peters and Waterman? The answer to this question is largely 'no.' Atari failed to develop and bring to market new competitive products; DEC deviated from its core business by branching out into a host of other markets; while Wang did the opposite and stayed too close to its roots when the market around it was changing.

Ingersoll-Rand, which did not make it into the category of excellence, successfully followed a middle ground. It is still in business today because it recognized the need to go beyond its core products (of heavy machinery), and expand into commercial products. As a result of this decision Ingersoll-Rand turned in revenues of USD 8.7 billion for 2007, up from USD 6 billion in 2003.[6]

What these cases suggest is that the recipe for excellence is not as excellent as Peters and Waterman's bestselling success might be seen to imply.

One reason for this is that the formula for excellence rests on eight factors and *only* those eight—leaving neither room for other variables that may have been instrumental to the success of a particular company, nor room for any residuum to be addressed. The mere fact that the eight factors identified can be attributed to the 43 companies that were deemed excellent in the late 1970s does not mean that these were the exact factors paving the way for their success. Rather, an X factor had played a part in many cases, without being identified by the authors; the proof of the pudding being that companies excluded from the authors' list went on to be very successful, while those that had been held up as model businesses failed within a very short timeframe.

Peters and Waterman's underlying assumption—that the correlation between the presence of these eight factors and a company's success is perfect—is made despite it being commonly known within statistics that correlation does not equal causality. That is to say, the success of these 43 companies could just as well be attributed to different or additional variables, which may be heterogeneous in the sense that each company has followed its *own* recipe to achieve success and gain a competitive advantage.

Other criticisms were levied at the book too. Some suggested that 'excellence' was oversimplified and trendy, though managers saw little to criticize in the prescription for success, and rushed to be excellent. When the popular business press began to point out the less-than-excellent performance of some of the 'excellent' companies, even managerial proponents had to acknowledge that perhaps the emperor was naked. One West Coast bumper sticker proclaimed "I'd rather be Dead than Excellent."[7]

Clearly there were shortcomings in the findings of *In Search of Excellence*. Although presented as a recipe for success, it did not stand the test. The lasting impact however was that others were now inspired to look for alternative formulae for success.

BUILT TO LAST BUT NOT NECESSARILY TO STAY AHEAD

If *In Search of Excellence* was the management book of the 1980s, then *Built to Last: Successful Habits of Visionary Companies*, written by two Stanford professors Jim Collins and Jerry Porras,[8] was unquestionably the management book of the 1990s, with sales to date topping 3.5 million copies.

Collins and Porras compiled a list of visionary companies by asking a representative sample of 700 CEOs to name up to five companies they perceived to be highly visionary. The CEOs themselves were chosen from Fortune 500 industrial companies, Fortune 500 service companies, Inc. 500 private companies and Inc. 100 companies. The responses were used to create a list of 18 companies that were most frequently named as visionary companies and which had outperformed the general market in terms of stock returns.

Published in 1994, the book paired the 18 visionary companies that had performed extremely well over a long period of time with peers that had been founded in the same period. These were companies that carried similar products and operated in similar markets, which fewer CEOs had listed in their responses, and which had shown a good but not excellent performance. By performing this paired comparison, the authors were able to identify patterns and develop an overarching premise for what it takes to build a visionary company, as well as associated management behaviors.

Put simply, the conclusion was that the visionary companies were those that had been able to preserve the core ideology of the company while simultaneously stimulating and continuously driving progress. The means by which this was achieved, which differentiated the visionary companies from their selected peers, were grouped into the five categories described in Table 2.1.

In contrast to the list of companies presented in Peters and Waterman's *In Search of Excellence*, all of those companies identified by Collins and Porras still exist to this day, making it hard to argue with the fact that they were, or are, built to last.

Their ability to outperform the market, however, was not a lasting feature for all of the visionary companies documented as companies such as Ford, Merck, Motorola, Sony, and Walt Disney have since experienced some difficulties and performed below the S&P 500 index when measured from 1994 onwards.[9]

Again, the notion that a clearly defined set of factors—and only these—are the cause for success is used to explain why some of those companies, labeled as 'visionary', subsequently encountered problems. But correlation does not equal causality so the factors presented may well be *attributable* to a visionary company but not necessarily the basis for its success.

ONE PLUS ONE EQUALS NONE

That a generic recipe for success rests on a defined number of variables is as likely as the alchemist's transmutation of common metals into gold. An indication of this is the fact that many of the same companies have been used as role model companies in both *In Search of Excellence* and *Built to Last*.

A quick comparison of the companies included in these two publications reveals that 16 companies feature in both, as highlighted in Table 2.2. As can

Table 2.2
Companies Common to *In Search of Excellence* and *Built to Last*

Common Companies	In Search of Excellence	Built to Last
3M	Excellent	Visionary
Boeing	Excellent	Visionary
Bristol-Myers	Non-Excellent	Non-Visionary
Burroughs	Non-Excellent	Non-Visionary
General Electric	*Non-Excellent*	*Visionary*
General Motors	Non-Excellent	Non-Visionary
Hewlett-Packard	Excellent	Visionary
IBM	Excellent	Visionary
Johnson & Johnson	Excellent	Visionary
Marriot	Excellent	Visionary
Merck	Excellent	Visionary
Procter & Gamble	Excellent	Visionary
Texas Instruments	*Excellent*	*Non-Visionary*
Wal-Mart	Excellent	Visionary
Walt Disney	Excellent	Visionary
Westinghouse	Non-Excellent	Non-Visionary

be seen here, only two of these 16 companies (General Electric and Texas Instruments, shown in italics) receive a different label from one publication to the other in terms of their performance. So how come 14 out of 16 companies achieve success by following markedly different recipes?

Once again, no allowance has been made for the influence of an 'X factor.' *Built to Last* therefore assumes the same fallacy as *In Search of Excellence*, that following the recipe is assumed to lead automatically to company success.

One might wonder which recipe, if any, these companies actually subscribe to, or if they combined the findings of the two publications to arrive at a master plan. Perhaps they devised their own recipe for success. What can be concluded with a reasonable degree of certainty, however, is that one generic recipe leaves little room for another, so the very presence of two must add up to a total closer to none.

As if it were not enough to have two generic recipes for how to excel in business and outlast the competition, the new millennium saw the release of an additional two publications which have also received substantial success in terms of copies sold.

FROM GOOD TO GREAT TO EVERGREEN

Perhaps inspired by the two building blocks, *Big Hairy Audacious Goals* and *Good Enough Never Is*, one of the authors of *Built to Last*, Jim Collins, decided that a recipe for how to become a visionary company did not suffice. To remedy the situation he embarked on a project that sought to identify the factors that catapult a company from being good to becoming great.

Published in 2001, his book *Good to Great*[10] examines what it takes for companies to make the leap from ordinary to extraordinary. Its findings are based on the study of 1,435 companies that had been among the Fortune 500 companies during the period from 1965 to 1995. Of the 1,435, only 11 companies displayed the desired pattern of being average performers for 15 years followed by 15 years of exceptional performance, even beating the usual stars among high-performing companies such as 3M, Boeing, General Electric, Hewlett-Packard, and Procter & Gamble.

The author then identified a comparator company for each of the 11 great companies, which operated within the same industry and arguably had the same resources and opportunities, so that significant differences could be pinpointed. From this analysis of paired comparisons, Collins identified six characteristics (described in Table 2.1) as being instrumental in elevating companies from 'good' to 'great.'

In addition to the six characteristics, the concept of the 'fly wheel 'and the 'doom loop' were also introduced as illustrations of how the companies made the leap. It is argued that none of the companies that made the leap did so through a single defining action or grand scheme for turnaround, but instead reached greatness through constant movement—a strategy that was initiated long before the breakthrough was reached. This development is compared to that of a fly wheel slowly beginning to spin and continually gaining speed in order to eventually take off.

The doom loop is the opposite process, of multiple quick fixes geared towards creating a breakthrough which never actually materializes, and instead leads to doom as the course is frequently changed, creating an atmosphere of uncertainty within the company.

Few can argue with the identified six characteristics given their highly generic nature, which allows for endless interpretation. As such, many business leaders may look at these six characteristics and feel that they are common sense and the foundation for sound business decision making. But there is a danger in making such assumptions. By adhering to these qualities, few business leaders will doubt that they have the right people on board. Similarly they are unlikely to face the brutal facts of market movements, or pursue activities they do not think they are particularly good at or are not passionate about. This being the case, it is fair to assume that the same six characteristics may apply just as well to companies that never end up making the leap from good to great, and even to companies performing below average.

Interestingly, only one company—Philip Morris—can be found in the lists of both 'visionary' companies presented in *Built to Last* and 'great' companies identified in *Good to Great*.

How can this be? Does this imply that the recipe for how to become a visionary, enduring, and high-performing company is different from the recipe that will catapult you to greatness? The short answer offered by Collins is 'yes.'

Despite *Good to Great* being the more recent publication to be penned by Jim Collins, the author argues that it precedes *Built to Last* in terms of when the two recipes are or should be applied. First, a company will apply the ideas set out in *Good to Great* in order to transform the business from the obscurity of being an average performer. Thereafter the company will apply the lessons of *Built to Last* to sustain this achieved greatness. This dual-pronged approach is illustrated in Figure 2.1.

What this suggests is that the recipe for success changes depending on the situation a given company finds itself in. Different measures must be used for different circumstances, supporting the premise that no generic recipe for success exists.

If the combined ideas presented in *Good to Great* and *Built to Last* are thought to represent such a recipe, would it not then be logical to assume that the ideas presented in other publications such as *In Search of Excellence* could be added too, in order to arrive at an even better mixture for success? If so, then the concepts and ideas presented in *all* strategy and management literature that seeks to identify the formula for success are merely lists of ingredients that the individual company can mix and match as they see fit. In the sample used we can find successful companies, yet cases such as Fannie Mae (which is among the 'good-to-great companies') illustrate the opposite.

Even a pick-and-choose list seems problematic. Should we pick all cherries or only a few cherries? How do we assess whether some cherries are better than others? And how does the X factor fit into the equation?

FIGURE 2.1 The Relationship Between *Good to Great* and *Built to Last*

DOES IT WORK?

The last example within management literature that we will draw on as yet another attempt to identify the one and only recipe for success is *What (Really) Works: The 4+2 Formula for Sustained Business Success*. Published in 2003, it was a result of what was called the Evergreen Project.[11] Three Harvard professors, William Joyce, Nitin Nohria, and Bruce Robertson, spearheaded the project, undertaking a study of 160 companies and their performance across two different periods of time—the first from 1986 to 1991, and the second from 1991 to 1996. The 160 companies were selected on the basis of total return to shareholders, a market capitalization of between USD 100 million and USD 6 billion, and representation of 40 narrowly defined industries, each providing four companies for analysis.

Using total return to shareholders as the measure, the 160 companies were divided into four categories based on their performance over the two periods, as displayed in Table 2.1.

Following this categorization, more than 200 management practices, of both broad and specific nature, that were thought to influence business success, were analyzed with the purpose of identifying which of these could be correlated with the winning companies.

This analysis identified two sets of management practices a company must adhere to in order to ensure a high return for its shareholders. The first is a set of primary management practices that a company must excel at in order to achieve success, supplemented with a second set consisting of secondary management practices of which the company must excel in at least two out of four characteristics. The 4+2 formula for sustained business success became a reality, covering the management practices in 160 companies.

Unfortunately the 160 companies are not named, which makes it impossible to determine whether the formula did indeed work for these organizations. Nor are the 200+ management practices that went into the analysis communicated. As a result it cannot be determined whether those chosen were in fact the basis for success, or if there were others among the 200 that could have been argued to more directly contribute to success. This and the highly generic nature of the identified practices make it practically impossible to disagree with the findings of *What Really Works;* the missing data, meanwhile, are a cause for concern.

Again, the notion that this formula, or rather recipe, represents a generic roadmap for all companies wishing to achieve sustained success remains a point of disagreement. In this case, the recipe states that a company must excel at all four primary practices and at least two of the secondary ones. Once more, the correlation between the recipe and success is presented as being perfect. The implication is that no residual, undefined X factor is being called into play, albeit that some flexibility is granted at the secondary level where two out of the four parameters are 'optional.'

GREAT BY CHOICE

Jim Collins continues to devote his time to researching successful companies, and to trying to distill the new recipe for success. He began with *Built to Last*, continued with *Good to Great*, and has recently published his third book to offer a winning formula. This time he has collaborated with Morten T. Hansen, to craft and publish the bestseller, *Great by Choice*.[12]

This third book stands apart from his previous books through its focus on not just performance, but also on the type of unstable environments faced by leaders today. More specifically, Collins and Hansen have studied companies that have risen to greatness and beaten their industry indexes by a minimum of 10 times over 15 years. These results have been achieved in environments characterized by big forces and rapid shifts that are difficult for leaders to predict.

Among the key (new) findings in the study are the observations that:

- The best leaders were not greater risk-takers, more visionary or more creative than in comparative companies. However, they were more disciplined, more empirical, and more paranoid.
- Innovation alone turns out not to be the trump card in a chaotic world. Rather, the ability to scale innovation and to blend creativity with discipline are more significant.
- Acting according to the belief that leading in a fast-moving world always requires 'fast decisions' and 'fast actions' is a good way to get trapped and killed.
- The great companies changed less in reaction to a radically changing world than peer organizations.

The results of the study are being developed into a number of lines of thinking, frameworks, and practical concepts intended to be used as guidelines for companies and managers. Examples of these are included in the various chapters of the new book, with a view to determining what it takes to build a great organization with longevity.

It is interesting to reflect on the sample of companies included in the book. All seven are of US origin. The majority are operating worldwide. What is noteworthy too is that the study of the companies took place in the period 1967 to 2002 (the companies have a varied time-span) meaning that the findings are based predominantly on material and numbers from the past.

The authors are aware of the limitations of their study with respect to the time periods and the sample, although they appear confident that their conclusions have a certain sustainable value, and that the concepts distilled from their various former studies can increase the odds of building a great company.

The bottom line is that a recipe based on data that goes so far back in time might provide valuable inspiration, but has inevitable limits when applied to the brave new world in which companies are operating today.

THE MIX OF EXCELLENCE, HOW TO LAST, GREAT LEAPS, AND THINGS THAT WORK

Having discussed five different recipes for success that have appeared in the management literature over the past three decades, we would propose that there is no such thing as a definitive recipe for successful strategic stewardship of a company.

This is not to say that the management books discussed in the previous sections do not provide useful food for thought and good pointers on how to develop a business, and to potentially achieve success, or perceived success, but rather to stress the point that recipes do not guarantee success.

When comparing the ideas presented in each recipe, whether these are referred to as attributes, methods, characteristics, or practices (as shown in Table 2.1), it can be argued that these do not represent distinct sets of options but rather an à la carte menu from which business leaders are inspired to mix and match to achieve the transformation they seek.

This contention is supported by the fact that, to a large extent, the same companies are being used as case studies across the various publications. No fewer than 10 out of 18 companies dubbed 'visionary' in *Built to Last* can be found on the list of 'excellent' companies in *In Search of Excellence*, suggesting that these companies can be made to fit any of the formulae if so desired. The company, Philip Morris, features in both *Built to Last* and *Good to Great*, suggesting its model matches up with two generic recipes. It is possible that further replication exists too, but it is impossible to check given that a list of companies has never been published for the research behind the 4+2 formula expounded in *What Really Works*. In *Great by Choice*, Southwest Airlines, Intel, and Apple are among the examples cited. Incidentally, none of the companies from *Good to Great* are present in *Great by Choice*, although a fairly similar methodology is being used. It would be little cause for surprise if further repetition was found however.

TROUBLED WATERS

There are parallels between the cookbook approach to business management and strategy literature and its search for identifying the essential criteria of ultimate success, and the alchemist's hunt for the recipe for gold.

In the case of honing business strategy, this hunt has so far proved unsuccessful for a number of reasons. The main ones are summarized below:

1. As discussed, an unacceptably high number of the companies listed in the recipe books eventually fail. This is a critical point, as the performance of these companies—including Digital Equipment Corporation, Wang, Atari, and Fannie Mae—was used to identify the underlying recipe of successful companies.
2. Some of the same companies are used as working models to justify different recipes as visualized in Table 2.2. This was the case for companies like 3M, Boeing, Walt Disney, HP, IBM, Johnson & Johnson, Marriot, Merck, Procter & Gamble, and Wal-Mart in some of the older comparisons. Consider how many times Starbucks and Southwest Airlines too have been repeatedly referred to in recent business literature to support (different) recipes.
3. Fixed recipes leave no room for unexplained contributors (the role played by the elusive X factor). This implies that a considerable number of the prominent companies—including Apple, Hotmail, Google, Huawei, and Ryanair—would be left ignored by traditional strategy literature, despite being highly successful disruptive companies—because they don't fit the mold.
4. Agreed recipes pretend to see perfect correlation between their model and success. However, in reality they expose no perfect correlation. In an increasingly complex world it is naïve to suppose that vast numbers of interplaying elements could be reduced to a handful of clearly identifiable criteria for success.
5. No proof has been presented to justify the assumed cause–effect relationship between the recipes and success. Many other factors may influence the success of companies besides those assumed in the recipes, and in some instances it may even be that it is the intermediary success of a company that allows for the creation of a stronger culture, more resources expended on recruitment, or stay-close-to-the-customer programs.
6. Hidden and even unhidden problems in many of the successful companies are often not addressed. So when company leaders are asked to explain their success they often overemphasize the good stories and disregard failures.
7. A pervasive delusion—the so-called Halo Effect—takes over, so that company leaders and observers are blinded by positive performance (see Figure 2.2).
8. Best practice is difficult and sometimes impossible to transpose from one company to another.

Ultimately, success in the corporate world today cannot be reached by following a generic recipe for success.

The extensive reference to the same companies and the fact that each can seemingly be made to fit nearly any strategic approach is perhaps what prompted

The Halo Effect—The tendency for the performance analysis of a company to reflect only the overall results.

The Delusion of Correlation and Causality—Do we always know which thing causes what?

The Delusion of Single Explanation—There is rarely one specific factor that can explain everything.

The Delusion of Connecting the Winning Dots—It is impossible to isolate the reasons for being successful as most studies don't compare such organizations with less successful companies.

The Delusion of Rigorous Research—The data may lack the required quality.

The Delusion of Lasting Success—Sustainable formulae for success don't exist.

The Delusion of Absolute Performance—Company performance is always relative.

The Delusion of the Wrong End of the Stick—It may be true that successful companies pursue a focused strategy but this doesn't mean that a focused strategy always lead to success.

The Delusion of Organizational Physics—Company performance does not have the certainty of an immutable law of nature, so it cannot be predicted with the accuracy of the natural sciences.

FIGURE 2.2 The Nine Delusions Related to the Halo Effect[13]

Phil Rosenzweig to introduce the notion of 'the Halo Effect' (2007). Rosenzweig offers a sharp critique of current strategic thinking, arguing that it is pervaded by the tendency to offer specific evaluations based on general impressions—the Halo Effect. He lists nine delusions (see Figure 2.2) currently present in the literature as he sees them, and suggests that business managers should adopt an open-eyed, critical, and considered approach to strategy—rather than seeking the definitive recipe for success, as the majority of these are flawed.

PRESCRIPTIONS FOR STRATEGIC SUCCESS OR . . .?

Some of the characteristics depicted in the recipe literature on strategic management are taken up in a considerable number of other books prescribing approaches to corporate strategy.

The Game for Prescription

Commonly, prescriptions around (corporate) strategy tend to be rooted in either history of war, as typified by Clausewitz,[14] or economic theory, most notably the work of Adam Smith.[15] But it is reasonable to ask whether the challenges facing a global, 21st-century company will be best addressed by sending the troops (employees) into battles (against competitors) with a clear plan or prescriptive strategy. Or whether a company's strategic choices draw any parallels with rational choice between military options?

Whether this remains appropriate or not, the reality is that such themes continue to be heavily utilized to steer strategy and management.

War + Market Economy = Michael Porter

Michael Porter is a prominent proponent of battle and market economy metaphor in the pursuit of 'sustainable competitive advantage.'[16] His resulting 'recipe' remained largely undisputed for many years and almost became law. A number of terms from the strategy vocabulary have gained strength due to Porter's efforts too, such as 'market leadership,' 'first-mover advantage,' choosing an attractive industry, sticking to only one of the generic strategies, avoiding being 'stuck in the middle,' and many others.

Porter has been labeled as belonging to the positioning school or industry/ environmental theories of strategy, based on the assertion that organizations act entirely rationally and are driven by profitability.

Switching From External Focus to Internal Dedication

Where Porter dominated much of the conventional strategy thinking in the 1980s, the so-called resource-based theories of strategy gained a stronghold in the 1990s, arguably as a reaction against the heavy Porter-based emphasis on profit maximization in the 1980s. The organization's own resources are the starting point here; combining these can create competitive advantage, particularly if this is orchestrated in such a way that competitors are not able to imitate immediately.

Key to understanding the resource-based school of strategy is the view that the latter depends on learning, and that learning depends on capabilities. This way, crafting dynamic capabilities became crucial to achieving success, and subsequently much focus was attracted to the 'learning organization.' Briefly, the three most widespread concepts from Prahalad and Hamel's joint work became for companies to (a) rely on their 'core competencies'; (b) set a clear direction by way of 'strategic intent'; and (c) 'stretch and leverage' the limited resources at hand.[17]

Although Porter, Prahalad, and Hamel attracted much attention, there were also other theories with prescriptive elements in the conventional paradigm. One is the so-called 'game-based' theory which tries to optimize the selection of the best strategic option. Others include network-based theories, according to which some organizations can deliver better value to customers and create competitive advantage over rivals through cooperation with selected competitors.

My Bonnie Lies Over the Ocean

A more recent bestselling strategy book has been *Blue Ocean Strategy*.[18] The philosophy is contained in the subheading of the book, *How to create uncontested market space and make the competition irrelevant*. Notwithstanding the popularity of this book, the enthusiasm of this prescribed approach has faltered somewhat—simultaneously with the financial crises and the fact that some of the example companies fueling the theory (notably Starbucks) have since experienced setbacks. Some of the buzzwords are still within the framework of the conventional paradigm in the implicit 'blue ocean' recipe. Examples include the notion of uncontested market space, value creation through differentiation, and making competition irrelevant.

It Matters Now

In another work, *What Matters Now* (2012), author Gary Hamel[19] promotes a recipe on (as is encapsulated in the subheading) *How to win in a world of relentless change, ferocious competition and unstoppable innovation*. The recipe-like prescription assigns Hamel to the conventional paradigm, however in a subsequent chapter (Chapter 4) we will revert to some of the trajectories that propel Hamel from the conventional paradigm to the new, emerging paradigm.

In *What Matters Now* he considers the fundamental, make-or-break issues that will determine whether an organization 'thrives' or 'dives' in the years to come. The answer, according to Hamel, can be distilled down to five critical issues:

- ■ **Values**: With the trust in large organizations at an all-time low, there is an urgent need to rebuild the ethical foundations of capitalism. What's required is nothing less than a moral renaissance of business, Hamel says.
- ■ **Innovation**: Innovation is the only defense against margin-crushing competition, and the only way to outgrow a dismal economy ('Innovate or die'). In too many companies, innovation is still a buzzword, rather than the responsibility

of every individual. This must change. What is needed is an innovation movement or a democratization of the innovation phenomenon.

- **Adaptability**: In a world of accelerating change, every company must build an evolutionary advantage. The forces of inertia must be vanquished. The ultimate prize: an organization that is as nimble as change itself.
- **Passion**: In business as in life, the difference between 'insipid' and 'inspired' is a passion. With mediocrity fast becoming a competitive liability, success lies in finding new ways to rouse the human spirit at work; a reinvention of the way organizations care for their human resources.
- **Ideology**: Today, businesses need more than better practices; they need better principles. Bureaucracy and control have had their day (though are still quite present in many organizations). It is time for a new ideology based on freedom, democracy, and self-determination.

By subscribing to these elements, combined with six critical factors (anticipation, intellectual flexibility, strategic variety, strategic flexibility, structural flexibility, and resilience-friendly values), his book provides a blueprint for creating organizations that are fit for the future and fit for human beings.

The Conventional Paradigm Revisited

Most of the business books discussed to this point are based on either interviews with top managers, the stock performance of US companies, or a combination of both.

Notwithstanding the fact that many companies have gained very valuable insight into strategic thinking from these conventional textbooks, some limitations inevitably apply too. We have already laid out one of these, namely the fact that many of the concepts and recipes are based on research in which the Halo Effect is operating. It is well known that this creates (room for) bias because focus is placed on what went very well in the stewardship of a company (or what actually went wrong but was retold to appear successful). Focus is not on what is hidden under the carpet or on failures but rather on how a company became a first mover and subsequent market leader, and the 'best-practice' lessons that can be drawn from the organization under the spotlight.

It would seem that the incentive to convert failure to success, or to acquiesce with perceived success (rather than real success), has been too high. This incentive has also manifested itself during and since the financial crisis of 2008, as severe defects of stock option programs to top management in a number of countries became evident. When it comes to the notion of best practice, there has been evidence of a rush among CEOs to either pursue self-nominated 'best practice' or to greatly influence industry-specific analyses.

For the last 40 years, almost every leader in every company has professed unbounded zeal for learning from best practice. By association, this means they have focused their attention and energies disproportionately on *existing* knowledge. But existing knowledge is based on *past* performance, which presents an intellectual and methodological challenge when dealing with strategy which is *forward*-looking. In short, the conventional paradigm is overwhelmingly based on all the 'knowns,' whereas strategy needs to address all the 'unknowns.' We will return to this important distinction and its implications later on, particularly when describing the emerging new paradigm.

Before we do this, however, it is worth recapping the core components of the conventional paradigm. These can be summarized as in Table 2.3. As indicated in the right-hand part of the table, a recipe covering a number of recommendations typically applies.

The conventional paradigm has its own terminology which is widely accepted as a common body of knowledge. Table 2.3 only represents some selected examples of the terminology. However, as already fleshed out, this paradigm is deficient when it comes to the stewardship of today's companies. A new paradigm has not yet been established but is beginning to emerge[20] which we will address in the next chapter.

Table 2.3
Summarizing the Conventional Paradigm

Paradigm/Terminology	Conventional Paradigm
Market position	Market leadership
Starting block	First mover, pole position, and sustainable advantages
Change mode	Differentiate and value creation
Size of change	Marginal/incremental
Benchmarking technology	Best practice
Methodology	Analytical
Cost structure	Conventional cost structure
Degree of rationalization	Everything explained/planned
Market perfection	Market forces
Regulatory forbearance	Marginally or not addressed
Governmental support	Marginally or not addressed

KEY REFLECTIONS

A. Most conventional textbooks on management and strategy are based on examples of US stock-listed companies and their past (and in some cases present) performance. What limitations does this present when you try to extrapolate from and apply such literature?

B. An overwhelming number of recipes for success are offered. When these are used in practice, what precautions do you have to make if the contingencies and assumptions set out are different from the contingencies and assumptions in your organization?

C. The conventional paradigm deals with data and documentation which are already largely well known to you and to others. However, strategy addresses *future* actions and reactions in the medium to long term, where knowledge is often missing and where there are many unknowns. Which fallacies must you address in this context?

NOTES

1 This issue, of something akin to a perpetual wheel of 'quick fixes', has not been widely addressed in the literature but is part of Michael McGill's (1988) critique in *American Business and the Quick Fix,* and in Henry Mintzberg's (2005) *Managers Not MBAs: A hard look at the soft practice of managing and management development,* Berrett-Koehler, San Francisco.

2 We addressed this thoroughly as part of the research underpinning our book (2010) *Return on Strategy,* and the section on strategic management recipes as part of Chapter 2 represents to some extent a redrafting of this work.

3 Peters, Tom J. and Waterman, Robert H. (1982), *In Search of Excellence: Lessons from America's Best-Run Companies,* Harper & Row, New York, p. 22.

4 *Business Week* (1985), November 5.

5 http://en.wikipedia.org/wiki/atari

6 Form 10-K for the fiscal year ended December 31, 2007.

7 McGill, Michael (1988), *The American Business and the Quick Fix,* p. 24.

8 Collins, Jim and Porras, Jerry (1994), *Built to Last: Successful Habits of Visionary Companies,* Harper Business, New York.

9 Yahoo finance, charting the period from August 1994 to August 2008.

10 Collins, Jim (2001), *Good to Great: Why Some Companies Make the Leap . . . and Others Don't,* Harper Business, New York.

11 Joyce, William, Nohria, Nitin, and Roberson, Bruce (2003), *What (Really) Works: The 4+2 formula for sustained business success,* Harper Business, New York.

12 Collins, Jim and Hansen, Morten T. (2011), *Great by Choice,* Harper Business, New York.

13 Rosenzweig, Phil (2007), *The Halo Effect: . . . And the eight other business delusions that deceive managers,* Free Press, New York.

14 See e.g. Clausewitz, Carl von (1997 edition), *On War,* Wordsworth Edition, Herts., UK.

15 Smith, Adam (1976), *The Wealth of Nations,* edited by R.S. Campbell and A.S. Skinner, Glasgow edition of the Works and Correspondence of Adam Smith.

16 Porter, Michael has contributed several books, beginning with *Competitive Strategy* (1980, Free Press, New York), where the groundwork for analyzing industries and competitors was laid down with a clear recommendation to choose the most attractive industry. *Competitive Advantage* (1985, Free Press, New York) introduces a 'toolkit' for obtaining sustained competitive advantage.

17 The works of Prahalad and Hamel appeared e.g. in influential articles in *Harvard Business Review* and notably in Prahalad, C.K. and Hamel, G. (1994), *Competing for the Future,* Harvard Business School Press, Boston.

18 Kim, W. Chan and Mauborgne, R. (2005), *Blue Ocean Strategy: How to create uncontested market space and make the competition irrelevant,* Harvard Business School Press, Boston.

19 Hamel, Gary (2012), *What Matters Now,* Jossey-Bass, New York.

20 See n. 8, Chapter 1, where we try to be cautious when utilizing Kuhn's term paradigm concerning something which is not yet fully constituted and which is not as exact as e.g. a paradigm shift in natural sciences.

Chapter 3

How a New Paradigm Is Emerging

ON EMERGENCE

We saw in Chapter 2 that the conventional paradigm has considerable shortcomings. It is largely built on the basis of an existing common body of knowledge from which a number of strategic theories and terminology emanate.

A classic example is Michael Porter's approach, according to which a company has to choose among generic strategies—notably either a differentiator or a cost-leader type of strategy—and select an attractive industry to work in. Moreover, a number of recipes emerged with typically up to eight rules that must be strictly followed to achieve success. Both in the case of generic strategies in seemingly attractive industries, and in the case of recipes, we are dealing with normative thinking, as there is assumed to be a direct correlation between the rules of the recipe and success.

In this chapter we will take a closer look at an emerging paradigm, which dramatically alters the equations presented in the conventional paradigm. We start by looking into the notion of disruption, before going on to study the importance of the strategic mindset, both of which are important cornerstones to the emerging paradigm.

DISRUPTION AS A KEY STRATEGY DRIVER

Tomorrow's innovations do not show up in market statistics. They take the market by surprise. It is the same with disruption. When successful 'black swans' begin to disrupt, it is often too late for ducklings or even white swans to react.

After Apple introduced the iPhone, Nokia quickly lost its market leadership in the smartphone market of the industrially developed countries as well as its cash cow in feature phones.

Sabena, Swissair, and many other flagship airlines were similarly extinguished by discount carriers and in the same industry, young Emirates soon emerged as the largest carrier in the world, disrupting the notion of intercontinental flights with Dubai as the new epicenter.

In the telecoms market Huawei suddenly entered center stage, challenging the former incumbents. The question now is whether this aggressive ICT solutions provider will now also quash Ericsson, the former market leader among mobile vendors.

Rather than quashing them, Tata just swallows iconic brands one by one. Tata, from the once submissive India, has taken over Jaguar, Land Rover, Tetley, and others from UK, reversing imperialism with a new form of 'disruption from the bottom.'

What are the prospects of other successful black swans hatched in eggs in developing countries? Aravind of India is able to provide professional eye surgery for a fraction of services offered elsewhere and is the first major example of cost effectiveness when 'McDonaldizing' the health sector, representing extreme further disruptive potential. Natura, originating in Latin America, has founded the new concept of globalizing beauty, in the process taking market share and profitability from conventional peers. It is expected that many more companies from developing countries will emerge as black swans in the near future.

With this in mind we will now delve deeper into the notion of disruption before going on to consider the underlying mindset.

Historically, the notion of disruption relates to destruction.

Creative Destruction

Back in 1942, the economist Joseph Schumpeter conceived his theory of 'creative destruction' to explain how capitalism works on the premise of change: i.e. that new businesses are continually destroying old ones.[1] The sheer innovative power of humans leads to the creation of new ideas, new products, new processes—and the creators have no intention of waiting for the old-timers to adjust before they take the frontier. These change makers, or entrepreneurs, destroy in order to create. The notion of creative destruction ironically dates back to capitalism's ultimate opponent, Karl Marx, and his 1848 Communist Manifesto. In his theory, capitalism would ultimately destroy itself because of its need to destroy existing wealth just to create new wealth.

But when Schumpeter picked up the concept some 100 years later, he turned around the notion of destruction from an endpoint to a continuous fresh start for capitalism. In his view, the changes that create and recreate capitalism come from within the capitalist system itself, blowing 'gales of creative destruction' through corporate life and bringing with them qualitative revolutions which create radically new conditions for companies. The capitalist system and components then adapts to these, and the process starts over. In present-day capitalism, post financial crisis, post globe-shaking corporate scandals and certainly post the old industrial society, we are on the brink of such a qualitative revolution. The question is how will we manage these changes, and how can existing companies help create them and not just be blown away by their force?

Since Schumpeter conceived the idea of creative destruction, management research has probed further into its features, particularly the difference between those companies currently on top of the game, and the upcoming entrepreneurs that challenge the status quo and ultimately bring the reigning companies to fall.

The disruption literature in the wake of Christensen's *Innovator's Dilemma* (1997)[2] tried to classify what exactly it is entrepreneurs *do* to create disruptive innovations and change businesses and sometimes entire markets (see Table 3.1). A pivotal insight is the fact that disruptive entrepreneurs can afford a much lower profit margin than incumbents, since they have little overhead to manage. At the same time, they have no chance of competing in existing markets and must find new ways of competing. They can do this by creating new markets from scratch, or by creating a very low-end disruption in an existing market, hollowing out the pricing model of incumbents. The threat of the entrepreneurs is always there, and the far too often neglected question for incumbents is whether to attack them with an aggressive strategy to keep them from cannibalizing mainstream markets, or whether to cannibalize yourself and develop before others do it for you.

Tjan, Harrington, and Hsieh (2012)[3] have tabled a refreshing view on entrepreneurs. Instead of creating a recipe for success to become standard operating procedure, as in the conventional paradigm, they have looked into the various combinations of four attributes: Heart, Smarts, Guts, and Luck.

In so doing, the authors have created a tool to self-awareness, introspection, and self-improvement. Irrespective of the combination of attributes entrepreneurs had, they were high-risk takers and, in the words of the authors,

Table 3.1
Entrepreneurs versus Incumbents

	Complacent Incumbents	Proactive Entrepreneurs
Investment	Develop products and services currently in demand	Invest in the idea and future potential
Technology level	Focus on high-end improvements	Novel technologies underperforming at start
Initial customers	Mainstream	Fringe
Intended profit margin	Need for high profit margin to maintain company growth	Low profit margin initially
Market analysis	Market information through historic data	Tomorrow's markets through social data, exploration, big data

"they were all out to create some change, some disruption, something new."[4]

When change, disruption, and something new is compared with the conventional focus on business plans, it becomes clear that this book is one of the first movements towards a new paradigm.

Disruption Do's and Don'ts

As discussed earlier, there is plenty of advice for managers on how to develop winning strategies. The old-school advice from the disruptive innovation scholars was to build a special unit for change inside the organization. The argument was that it is so difficult for large corporations to change their systems, structures, strategies, and not least cultures that the most efficient innovation would need an entirely different unit to succeed. Hubs, labs, and spin-offs were the classic means of allowing organiza-

A. **Heart** (traits of idea-generation and cultural leadership). According to Tjan, Harrington and Hsieh's survey, 70% of founders with a subsequent successful exit started without a plan but were driven by their authentic vision, with passion as one of the code words. However, one of the shortcomings is that emotions override logic and judgment.

B. **Smarts** (traits of an architect and strategist). Smarts do not have a very high IQ but are above average. They are very good at conceptualizing and framing situations. However, one of the limitations is left-brain bias, in the sense that focus on details may imply missing the big picture.

C. **Guts** (general and implementer traits). High-performance drive and a sooner-rather-than-later approach mean a high score on execution. However, with 'checklist management' the broader aspiration may be missed.

D. **Luck** (traits of the opportunist and mentor/mentee). Giving and receiving ideas, counsel and relationships are a key strength, however with an overly laissez-faire approach at times.

tions to experiment with new products and approach new markets. But from our modern-day perspective of global interconnectedness, networked solutions and the power of new technologies such as social media, it seems somewhat naïve to want to create change through a small division isolated from the rest of the company.

When it comes to disruption created by aggressive companies pursuing a discount strategy, the distinction between the conventional thinking and the emerging new paradigm becomes evident. Companies providing clean-slate discounts are able to build up the entire organization around their core product, therefore allowing the entire organization to work on the same level playing field. As seen in the airline industry this clean-slate approach has generated carriers like Ryanair, EasyJet, South West Airlines, Emirates, and others, which have developed not only a very sound cost base but also a number of new, often innovative, approaches. This has allowed them to counteract Michael Porter's 'stuck in the middle' theory where you have to choose between a cost-leader strategy and a differentiator strategy.

In contrast, the incumbent airlines often tried to develop a shop-in-shop discount offering without major success. Either they cannibalized their own business or they were not able to compete with the clean-slate discounters. Scandinavian Airlines System's attempt to develop a low-cost brand, Snowflake, did not become successful. The Australian airline Quantas has chosen another route. It has a low-cost carrier as a part of the company. However this is operating totally separately from Quantas and under its own brand, Jetstar.

The implication is that the traditional oxymoron seems to wither away, driven by successful mixed strategies and/or new strategies. Innovative solutions seem to have been the glue in the airline industry which has made it possible for clean-slate companies to combine the best of a cost-leader and differentiator type of strategy.

Understand the Importance of the Periphery

To get new ideas and be a change maker, you need to look outside your habitat. The next leap forward cannot be expected to come from an organization's central group of managers; they are typically too embedded in their existing procedures, resources, and targets to offer a fresh perspective (although some may be innovative spirits, overflowing with game-changing solutions, they can still become too bogged down with structural detail to take their ideas forward).

The reality is that innovation has rarely come from the core, or from those in power, whether in business, politics, or cultural struggles. Innovation challenges the status quo and disturbs complacency and habit. As scholars and business people are increasingly arguing, to understand what's next one must look to the *periphery* of a company's current practices and operations. This sounds simple but what *is* the periphery, how do you search for it, and how do you know you've found it?

The periphery exists in everything that is not business-as-usual to the organization. It is less about a specific place or product than about insights and knowledge. The insights, questions, methods, and needs of all stakeholders traditionally not involved in core strategic decision making, all represent precious input to your understanding of what your business is missing or neglecting—and not least what it is capable of with the right people and mindset. These peripheral stakeholders can be just about anyone, and anywhere: fringe or new customers, corporate subsidiaries and emerging market offices, employees, suppliers, industry associations, competitors, scholars, communities, or governments.

Manage Complex Networks of Stakeholders

The insights from stakeholders at the periphery of your business of course do not simply materialize because top management talks with and listens to stakeholders. To truly harness the innovative power of these stakeholders, companies need to design structures and processes that can integrate knowledge with strategy. These processes must be flexible and involve the entire organization, so all employee groups can play a direct part in accessing, sharing, and developing information from other stakeholders.

Tomorrow's winners do not lock employees into rigid hierarchical systems and bureaucratic processes, but support their creative interplay with colleagues and external stakeholders. Across nations, markets, and business models, tomorrow's winners are those using novel technological platforms for collaboration around the organizational landscape of stakeholders. In this way, they build entirely new networks or ecosystems of stakeholders, in which all participants share knowledge and develop their specialties to match up with and capitalize on ever-developing networks.

Build Partnerships to Proactively Shape the Big Issues

Besides harnessing the potential of employees and their external networks, companies are increasingly entering cross-sector partnerships to address bigger issues. Disruption does not happen solely by competition; it is just as likely to occur as a larger phenomenon far beyond the influence of single companies. Resource limitations, social unrest, changing markets, and regulations are among such disruptors.

Take resources: the pace of modern-day economic growth puts intense pressure on the resources we need for consumption—from the most basic ones such as water and fossil fuels to more specific ingredients such as coltan (used in mobile phones) and palm oil (used in soaps, food, and a large variety of household supplies). One challenge for companies is the difficult political game of getting access to these resources which are geographically constrained. Almost half of the 50+ chemicals we need to keep up our current consumption pattern are in China, and some are found in war-ridden countries such as Rwanda and the Congo. Another challenge is their scarcity. The combination of these factors—access and scarcity—make it necessary to think smarter and more broadly than how to negotiate a good price for the company's next shipment of metals.

Companies need to conceive more sustainable and accessible alternatives, which is an enormous feat considering that most of our current societal structures are built on these finite resources. For nation states and governments, the resource agenda is equally poignant if our need for electricity, transport, and heating is to continue to be fulfilled in the not-too-distant future. Non-governmental organizations, interest groups, and political activists are also pushing for better management of the Earth's resources.

Resources, then, are yet another example of the many unknowns we have to deal with in the context of corporate strategy.

Experimenting With Products, Services, Processes, and Business Models

From the advice on periphery influences, networks, and partnerships detailed before, there is an underlying assumption that companies that listen, interact, and co-create will naturally be more innovative than their peers. But innovation requires something more than just interest and interaction. The most basic component—creativity—is much more demanding, more elusive, impossible to plan for and difficult to assess for return on investment. Innovation literature abounds with advice on creativity, and innovation front runners all work with creativity in one way or another. Obviously, creativity is vital in providing for unusual solutions in a world of constant disruption.

But creativity is full of uncertainty and coincidence. It requires playfulness and experimentation, and with this comes the courage to fail. Learning from failure is a topic that surfaces from time to time in business magazines and management literature, but we still know very little about how to cast failure in the development of strategies, products, and business models. Failure is still not part of most companies' external communication and stories about themselves. We have no idea how to measure failure, how we learn from it and what it drives. It is certainly not part of any corporate budget—it would be extremely unlikely to hear a CFO demand that X% of total budget should be spent on business-plan failure in an organization's Asian markets, for instance. Failure is still treated as a negative in corporate strategy.

Management Innovation Today

The types of innovations needed to create game-changing businesses do not come from internal innovation hubs, nor from neat procedures, or senior vice-presidents' yearly business strategies. Nor do they come from aggressive short-term growth and rush for shareholder satisfaction. Even more importantly, great products themselves will not fix the situation. It is the network and the ecosystems around innovations that create the deeper value—for the company and its customers, but also society at large. Increasingly, management scholars, and managers themselves are focusing on a broader picture, crammed with complexity and interactive features: the creation of value.

As some management gurus argue, companies and their investors have played the lead roles in the demise of the late industrial era. This has consequences—not just for all the stakeholders of each individual company, but also for the companies themselves. In the US for example, tough state regulation has had an impact on the freedom of business—as with the Sarbanes–Oxley Act that was enacted in 2002 in response to Enron and other large corporation scandals in the early 2000s. Had companies themselves operated with greater dignity, responsibility, and values, such strong and costly regulation could have been avoided. This is even more the case as we try to survive in the quagmire following the financial meltdown of 2008, which came as a sudden and unexpected event to almost all (making it one of the unknowns we have been talking about).

Besides a global recession and the bankruptcy of innumerable businesses, small and large, the consequences have again been regulatory. We see this in the American Dodd–Frank Act (2010), the hardest regulation of financial institutions and instruments since the Great Depression of the 1930s. Another example is the incessant issuing of austerity packages to save European economies, which hollows out investment opportunities for companies in desperate attempts to turn around plummeting national fortunes. So if companies and the institutions surrounding them do begin to depart from the conventional approach, according to which you can plan on a rational basis in the known universe, they will get in trouble. They need to consider the emerging new paradigm now—that which takes into account the as yet unknowns. Put another way, they need to cease being blind to their own blindness.

As described earlier, *innovation* is changing from having to do with singular outstanding product development conceived by a mastermind in the R&D department, to being based on great design, and "less about genius than empathy," as Hamel notes. He argues that by using empathy to understand customers, every company can learn to develop new products and services to their requirements. Examples of this inclusive customer orientation are many and varied. Apple, which seems unmovable from its number 1 position in rankings such as FastCompany's *The World's 50 Most Innovative Companies*, proves this again and again. Understanding that its customers want more than a standardized product, Apple combines its beautiful design with customer creations. Its revolutionizing App Store gives all customers the opportunity to design and buy add-ons to the software. Everybody is invited, and apps range from complex programs designed by professional agencies, to home-based nerds, and tech-wizzes' simple installations and games. As Hamel amusingly puts it, Apple "locks up customers with velvet handcuffs."[5] Its understanding and inclusion of customers prompts loyalty over freedom. Customer empathy generally opens up the innovation process to encompass much more than the product itself. The services and processes enveloping the product are equally, if not more important, before, during, and after the customer's purchase or core engagement with the product.

To make innovation possible in our time of capitalist transformation, *adaptability* is another essential component. The pace of change taking place in the global corporate landscape seems to be increasing exponentially, and although change has always been a premise for companies, there is no doubt that globalization has taken this up several gears. To create impact in such a world of impermanence, and not be swept away by it, companies need to develop flexibility as never before. This calls for cyclical strategizing where experimentation is turned into learning, and learning is analyzed in the light of business potential—after which selected potentials are invested in and meticulously processed and structured to become new products or services. This happens continuously and simultaneously in companies with a strong future.

But how does a company think, talk, and act in a flexible manner? What are the strategic hotspots that the future-embracing manager must pay attention to? First, managers and their organizations should turn to their individual and collective minds and, in the words of Hamel, challenge assumptions, create debate, and encourage dialectic thinking. Also, corporate management should not just imagine, but also rehearse the future—and set bold targets, as encapsulated in the phrase to 'put a man on the moon' echoing J.F. Kennedy's famous space program of the 1960s. More technically, companies can use strategic tools such as internal funding for new initiatives, future portfolios, and social media and platforms that invite collaborative efforts.

Understanding Deeper Values

If we now move on from adaptability and innovation, and look to Hamel's remaining three themes for modern managers, we find such un-managerial notions as *values, passion*, and *ideology*. In recent years management scholars and practitioners have been expanding the realm and understanding of strategy.

One of the insights is that the structural capabilities that companies need to produce and sell their products and services have become *standard:* an increasingly educated global workforce gives access to skilled labor and high-quality expertise. Supply chain management and distribution systems have more or less global standards. Internet-based meta-systems enable ready collaboration and information exchange with everyone from suppliers and customers to investors. This all makes business easier and allows for more efficiency and, ultimately, lower costs for the consumer.

What's left is all the stuff that money can't buy. For example the ability to truly gain value e.g. in *collaboration* with suppliers (= true partnership) rather than just in a transactional relationship with them. Or to use recycled raw materials instead of expensive and restricted extractive resources, and thereby save money and time *and* enhance brand value. Or to be able to truly harness the power of every single employee in the company—not by ensuring that they meet their narrow performance targets, but by involving them in the strategic improvements and visions of the company. In order to gain the competitive advantage and work satisfaction of such approaches to business, managers need to connect to their *humanity* and, with it, the above notions of values, passion, and ideology.

'Meaningfulness' is on the rise, and with it an understanding that business value is so much more than buying at a low price and selling with a profit. Value is a deep and sophisticated network beneath our economic organization worldwide. And every company is part of this network, whether they like it or not. This is in contrast to what one of today's prime spokesmen for a renewal of capitalism, author and manager Umair Haque, calls 'deep debt.'

Deep debt designates industrial-era capitalism with its rush for short-term gains and fierce exploitation of human and natural resources. Deep debt is the true cost of our products, when we add up all its factors. Though a product such as a burger may on the surface cost only USD 1 to produce and USD 2 to buy, this figure does not take into account factors such as the water consumption needed to produce the paper in which it is wrapped, the CO_2 footprint of the shop that sells it, the underpayment of the tomato-pickers, the obesity problems of many of its customers, and so forth.

If you add up all the negative factors and all the positive factors in the entire value cycle of the burger, the price would typically be much higher. This is deep debt—the debt we cannot, and do not want to see. Umair Haque[6] traces a direct line between deep debt and our enactment of *creative destruction* up to now, stating: "Capitalism is founded on the equation of creative destruction. The cornerstones of capitalism as we know it systematically and chronically undercount the costs of destruction and overcounts the benefits of creation. Undercounting destruction and overcounting creation [has] led to overdestruction and undercreation."[7] This inevitably becomes a costly affair for each company—its deep debt catches up sooner or later in the form of excessive resource expenses, angry customers, expensive lobbying costs, and so forth.

For companies that want to shape tomorrow, and enjoy it instead of stressfully exploit it, the alternative is deep value. Haque has identified a number of cornerstones for tomorrow's constructive capitalists. These are: (1) Value cycles (whereas the industrial-era capitalism's cornerstone was Value chains); (2) Value conversations (instead of formerly Value propositions); (3) Philosophies (instead of Strategies); (4) Completion (instead of Protection); and (5) Betters (instead of Goods).[8] The companies able to identify the deeper values of their products, adeptly involving the corresponding stakeholders, will harness better returns and grow new knowledge and techniques. They will all be producing not just *goods* to consume, but *betters:* "bundles of products and services that . . . have a tangible, meaningful, enduring positive impact" on people and societies. Tomorrow's winners have deep value ingrained in their mission, and their profits and shareholder value are simply benefits of their ability to produce something meaningful for others.

Management innovation is the hub of all other innovation, and though it comes in many shapes and sizes, and involves technology and tools, its core is the attitude behind it: the values, passion, and ideology that Hamel has advocated, and that thousands of managers are already putting to use. Some examples of this follow.

Innovation and Destruction—Two Sides of the Same Coin?

Innovation today faces daunting challenges, since it must not just transform companies towards more flexible and holistic ways of operating and strategizing, but must transform our entire notion of business itself. Transforming the management discipline is not a revitalization project; it is a revolution of thought. The scholars and managers involved in this project are only at the very beginning of it: they experiment with new ways of understanding of what business is and can be, with expanding the boundaries of business, with more flexible tools and structures, and more value-creating visions and strategies. It is exciting, it's invigorating, and it's necessary—but is it enough?

Based on our studies and lifelong work with companies in roles as diverse as managers, researchers, owners, and consultants, we wonder. There is no doubt that management and strategy is changing, and that the will to create deeper and better value is present in many management teams. However, even when the right intentions and expertise are fully ingrained in business transformation processes, we repeatedly observe companies and their managers being caught off-guard by changes happening around them.

Though strategy and management practice, as exemplified above, embrace flexibility and proactivity, there is still some way to go to make the revolution come alive. As both Gary Hamel and Umair Haque have argued, the new paradigm of capitalism, and with it strategy and management, will be just as big a game-changer as the industrial revolution was to the feudal society from which it sprung. When Adam Smith imagined the power of capitalism and merchants in 1776, trade and business was still regulated by guilds, power was in the hand of nobility and the Church, and common people lived in small households and served their local lords by tending to the land. He saw a world that did not yet exist, and the disruptions it would create and be created by. Some 250 years later, we need to do the same thing. We need to conceive of a world we cannot imagine, and begin to act on this vision. We need to move from the known to the unknown universe.

THE NEW MINDSET: WHEN BLACK SWANS FLY

To accommodate an emerging paradigm shift is in itself to embrace change. One of the key drivers of the emerging paradigm is change; constant, relentless change. The world is becoming ever more interconnected; factors and instigators of change have multiplied by thousands over the last decades. Companies and organizations all over the world are trying to explore and exploit the changes they can see around and ahead of them. Still, imagining a world completely different from the one we know, let alone creating strategies that will accommodate to such a world, is not exactly what most companies spend their time on.

In this context it is interesting to address the fact that far too many managers and companies display a mindset directed towards a world that doesn't exist any longer, or that may never have existed. Black swan companies, and the managers behind these, display a completely different mindset.

The Big Picture

As we described at the beginning of this chapter, disruption is not just something that companies do; it also implies the continuous and large-scale changes to which we as human beings, and our way of organizing ourselves, must adapt. The Economist Intelligence Unit (EIU) has identified three overarching groups of disruptors,[9] each with their specific forces and features: Resource disruptors, Policy disruptors, and Market disruptors (see Table 3.2).

The three groups of disruptors identified by the EIU reflect what companies must face and deal with today, and most managers would probably not question this list. As a matter of fact these disruptors are not even surprises anymore; they denote a future that is already here. EIU's disruptors are identified and imagined within the boundaries of the EIU's vision—a vision based on a strong market and financial understanding. The next step, however, is to imagine disruptions that are less obvious than these.

How to See What Does Not Yet Exist?

Statistician, author, and former stock trader Nassim Nicholas Taleb believes that our current understanding of disruption is naïve. In his book, *The Black Swan*,[10] he argues that disruption has become the norm. Yet as human beings we still act as if stability were the norm and disruption a kind of special event that happens and then ends, so we can return to stability. But those days are over, says Taleb. Disruption is the norm, not the deviator—and, more importantly, we cannot identify it in advance, as for example the Economist Intelligence Unit did above. It is more disruptive than that.

To explain what disruption is, and how it shapes our world, Taleb works with the concept of the two worlds, *Extremistan* and *Mediocristan*. Human beings generally live in Mediocristan. Here, we predict the future according to the mean, and according to what we already know. We plan and make strategies on

Table 3.2
Economist Intelligence Unit's Three Disruptors

Resource disruptors	Natural resources	Access is limited because of nationalization, regional instability, and overexploitation
	Human resources	Education globally is not at pace with corporate needs (or nation state needs, for that matter).
	Financial resources	Access to finance has shifted. The financial crisis has limited access for many, while others gain leverage through private equity and sovereign wealth funds, e.g. the Gulf states and China.
Policy disruptors	Transparency and accountability	National and transnational regulation put new requirements on corporate reporting and governance systems.
	Corporate responsibility requirements	Climate change, resource scarcity, fair trade/ eco movements, recycling needs, etc. oblige responsible companies that understand their 'corporate citizenship'.
	Operational complexity	The sheer multitude of markets and social, regulatory, and political environments in which companies operate, makes operations large and complex and puts pressure on management.
Market disruptors	Growth and decline of markets and economies	Large-scale fluctuations with China as the most obvious example. Having first impacted corporate production (outsourcing and moving production sites) and supply chain management, China is now growing as a market in its own right, in which every large player wants to sell. Meanwhile the attractiveness of producing in China decreases due to increasing local salaries.
	Geopolitical instability and change	Political changes, not just in economies such as the Arab countries, Russia, and China, but also in Western economies, impact business opportunity. For example the European Union's harsh financial regulations in 2011–12 to combat the downfall of the euro, and the precluding and following bankruptcy of numerous banks and businesses.
	New customers in rural and low-income mass markets	Serving customers in new markets involves different market intelligence methods, different products, different distribution systems—and the incumbent Western corporations may not be the winners of that game.

the basis of what we are able to observe and what we already know, and then we extend that to what we can't see and don't know. In Extremistan, the future erupts without following any defined logic; you cannot plan for it. It is like the probability of the occurrence of a black swan: things or events that are not supposed to be, but which nevertheless suddenly show up on our radar.

Our market economies are built on principles from Mediocristan. We gather data, tons of data, and process it in big systems, and use it to figure out the probability of outcomes and scenarios. The numerous statistical models for doing this help us process this data and help us believe that we *can* predict and even control the future. The problem is, building on methods such as the Bell Curve (see Figure 3.1), that they direct our attention to a theoretically derived mean, rather than to the many factors of reality that make outcomes random and created by outliers and not neatly calculable means and deviations.

The Bell Curve captures Mediocristan, Taleb says. Based on factors we already know, we try to understand the as yet unknown. The invention of the electric light, the nuclear bomb, and the World Wide Web are examples of inventions that could hardly have been foreseen by most people. The bloody revolts in Lebanon and Syria are others. The financial crisis following the bankruptcy of Lehman Brothers is another. Interestingly, Taleb gives credit to the US Secretary of Defense under the George W. Bush administration, Donald Rumsfeld, for his words on how to strategize for the unknown.

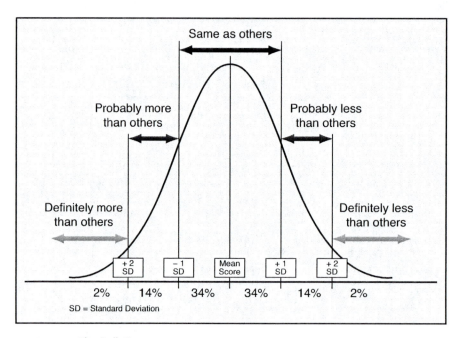

FIGURE 3.1 The Bell Curve

Human beings and our organizations are not geared to the unknown unknowns, though these increasingly rule our world to a considerable extent.

This is what Taleb's Extremistan is all about. So how can we become better at living in Extremistan—at understanding, embracing, and creating the unknown unknowns? First of all, we need to shake loose from our attachment to linear causality and short-sighted cause-and-effect thinking. Then we need to replace it with work that takes time, does not deliver immediate results, and is founded on intellectual, scientific, and artistic activity. The trouble is, "our emotional apparatus is designed for linear causality," Taleb notes.[11] We favor quick results; what is visible, over process which is less visible. This also means that many results of minor importance are favored over indefinite waiting for large results of major importance. When the large results hit us with a blow to our Bell-Curved vision, we are surprised and react to them to the best of our abilities. But how could we—as individuals, members of society, and corporate managers—turn around these surprises to make them something we can interact with, or even something we can ourselves be conscious creators of?

One thing is certain: if we want to harness the power of Extremistan, we cannot rely on the rational and functionalistic methods of the past few centuries. They have brought our societies and organizations far, and should not be discounted, but in an interconnected world of relentless change they need to be grounded in deeper and more human territory. We equate this ground to what Taleb calls "intellectual, scientific and artistic activity," or what Hamel describes as values, ideology and passion (as discussed earlier in this chapter).

So how do we connect with it?

Taleb's line of thinking is not entirely new. As far back as 1980, D.M. Hawkins published his *Identification of Outliers*, introducing the following definition of an outlier:[12]

> An outlier is an observation which deviates so much from the other observations as to arouse suspicions that is was generated by a different mechanism.

Unfortunately, this has generally been applied in management sciences to mean that the manifestation of an outlier is irrelevant and should be dismissed.

A study by Markus Paukku and Liisa Välikangas[13] documents this unfortunate trend by way of simply searching for outliers in the electronic archives of leading management journals (*Academy of Management Journal, Strategic Management Journal, Research Policy, and Journal of Management Studies*). The surprising facts are recounted in Table 3.3.

Essentially this statistical extract highlights that, even when outliers are registered, they are either ignored or dismissed in over 90% of cases. Interestingly, these figures have been compiled based on cases where outliers are mentioned,

Table 3.3
'Outlier' Analysis of Management Journals (from Paukku and Välikangas)

	Articles	Percent
Outliers mentioned	198	100
"Eliminated or controlled for"	147	74
"Noted as important" but not studied	34	18
Outliers studied	16	8

so there would be a number of additional instances of potentially relevant outliers. One category could be 'known unknowns', i.e. cases where the researcher knows that there are outliers operating but simply ignores finding them. Another could be where it is unknown to the researcher that outliers exist, e.g. because the researcher is blind to these valuable, yet unrecognized, phenomena.

In his book *Blindsided*,[14] sales manager, publisher, and author Jonathan Gifford argues that we need to do two things to make practical progress. First, we need to cultivate the non-rational side of our brains; second, we need to overcome our inclination to react unthinkingly to external events with emotions such as fear and greed.

But what is the alternative? To wait to cultivate the non-rational *and* to overcome emotional reactions? That seems contradictory.

Later, we will show that what human beings believe to be rational behavior is often something less cool and calculated, but driven instead by underlying emotions and flock behavior. This prevents us from understanding the broader perspective of our observations and actions, and from adopting a long-term view of the consequences. The implication is that we are unable to think beyond our existing norms and behaviors, and therefore fall prey to disruptions by people, phenomena, and organizations outside our control.

Jonathan Gifford argues that human beings' desire for better and richer lives also drives sometimes reckless behavior. We engage in rushes, bubbles, and revolutions to achieve something better for ourselves. This creates prosperity and new societies, as have gold rushes and land rushes for example. It creates economic progress through increased production and consumption, and it creates new societies and systems of welfare. But on the flipside of the rushes and bubbles are their human, social, and environmental costs. From the US land rushes of the 1930s to the dot.com and finance bubbles of the turn of the millennium, people pay a high price for development. Many factors come as a surprise to people participating in rushes, and the 'promised land' is not as golden as the hype surrounding it. When a new invention, investment type or quick way to prosperity gains momentum we embrace it because we want to believe we can make a better future for ourselves. But we are not capable of assessing its value from all perspectives.

Human beings *want* to be fooled, Gifford argues, because we want to believe that we have found the recipe for gold. This chimes perfectly with our findings in Chapter 2 where we noted that most of the literature on strategy and management is based on recipes. Alarmingly, many CEOs, MBA consultants, and board directors are 'fooled' into believing they have found the recipe for gold. In our experience, managers have an almost religious propensity to follow and defend their chosen recipe.

One thing is that your mindset is focused on following a recipe religiously; another is what you miss in the process. Gifford's summary of the situation is captured in the adjacent box.[15]

There is value-*destroying* disruption and value-*creating* disruption. We have advocated that the way in which a new capitalist paradigm can be opened is through value-*creating* disruption. But, as Umair Haque contends, value creation is a much deeper and more sophisticated game than value exploitation and destruction. We will dig deeper into the methods needed for this game in the coming pages, when we begin to discuss the strategic mindsets behind value-creating disruption.

> What we experience as rational decision-making is driven by impulses and urges of which we are barely aware; an overwhelming urge to take what is available now before someone else gets it; an inbuilt tendency to follow the herd; a strong sense of what is equitable and fair; an instinct to trust our own group and to be hostile to outsiders; a poor capacity for remembering disasters and planning for their reoccurrence; difficulty in envisaging the collective effect of our individual actions. These unexamined motivations are what cause us to be blindsided—to be surprised and distressed, at some future point, by the consequences of actions that we thought we had made rationally and dispassionately.
>
> (Gifford 2012: 222–223)

Before that, a note on what the destructive and short-sighted type of disruption actually costs us.

To give a final and more corporate example, we can consider the economic short-sightedness that appears to rule in Wall Street's investment banks, as documented in *Liquidated* and in the *New York Times* debate following "Why I am leaving Goldman Sachs."[16]

Here, analysts are seen to learn that advising customers is about getting the biggest profit out of the deal. The tools can be large and sophisticated financial models, investment portfolios, industry scenarios, and more. There is nothing wrong with the tools, but when the values treasured by senior management are all about making big money for the company, the tools become means to that end—and not to strengthening the long-term business of the corporate clients.

This has different levels of consequences. One is the immediate issue of discontent, as was seen when an executive director at Goldman Sachs quit his job with a fiercely critical article in the *New York Times*. In it he wrote: "It makes me ill how callously people talk about ripping their clients off." The opinion piece sparked a great debate about the culture at Goldman Sachs and other investment banks, and some of the immediate effects were a tarnished image and a growing recruitment challenge. The finance sector's recruitment numbers have plummeted since the financial crisis. In 2008 the number of Harvard seniors entering the finance sector was 28%, in 2011 it was 17%; meanwhile students rank investment banks lower and lower on their lists of places they would like to work.

The more medium-term effects may be losing customers. As the deserting executive director put it, "It astounds me how little senior management gets a basic truth: if clients don't trust you they will eventually stop doing business with you. It doesn't matter how smart you are." This kind of twisted knowledge is, of course, particularly alarming given how much time senior managers spend operating within the known universe. The result is that their mindset becomes more than usually distorted.

The long-term effects of seemingly reckless behavior of Goldman Sachs and other Wall Street organizations are less tangible, because as we have argued, future disruption is hard to identify with current experience and methods. But by looking at current trends, comparing with what history at large tells us about how much societies can change, and imagining what a more sophisticated capitalism could look like, the long-term risk scenario for investment banks could be downright scary. They might simply not exist in a hundred years' time, or at least their foundational short-term growth objectives might look completely different.

New kinds of corporate structures are on the rise, which avoid the traditional shareholder structure and the trading risks this involves. Family-owned companies are not just dusty old businesses but a way of gaining self-control—and interest in family-owned structures among scholars is strong. New companies emerge where the social mission and the profit mission are co-dependent. Even some big companies are pushing back at the 'quarterly capitalism' model that requires businesses to be managed exclusively for short-term shareholder value.

ON THE NEW STRATEGY MINDSET

Human beings can change! We can change our behavior, our methods, our organizations, and societies, and we have proved over the centuries that we can do this pretty quickly, too. In terms of companies and organizations, the entire field of strategic management is dedicated to facilitating change (which is the whole idea of strategy) and to making change possible (execution). In all the expert advice we have reviewed thus far, managers are encouraged to become more flexible, more creative, more innovative, more value driven, to listen better to their internal and external stakeholders, to create networks instead of hierarchies, in short: to become more agile. And there are countless great examples out there of the successes with one or more of these management methods and philosophies.

At the same time, however, it is also clear that the advocated transformations are not transpiring all that rapidly.

Change Is Easier Thought Than Done: Cases of Lost Incumbents

Even the most successful and long-lived companies may decline and ultimately die. In January 2012, the world's most famous photography company, Eastman Kodak, filed for bankruptcy after 134 years in business. Many conclusions can be derived and analyzed from the Kodak story, but the simplest version is the failure of the company to transform from film to digital cameras. It was too slow in realizing the pace of the digital revolution, and too reluctant to give up what had always been its core product: film. Strangely, it has been argued that Kodak was one of the companies with most insight and knowledge in the digital world. The problem was that it didn't manage to transform this knowledge into profitable business in a world which is changing more rapidly than ever and where black swans are all around.

Nokia, which we have touched on already, presents a more recent example. Just a few years ago, the mobile phone pioneer and long-time market leader was still one of those ideal case studies held up for inspection in business innovation literature and as a model for global corporate strategy. If the world had stood still in 2006–2007, Nokia would still be market leader today. But Nokia's strategic mindset did not take into account what Richard Rumelt labels the "smooth-sailing fallacy,"[17] where people assume that a lack of recent tremors and storms means that there is no risk.

The same was the case with Research in Motion (the creator of BlackBerry). Indeed, the list of big companies that have failed to successfully adapt to market disruption is unending. Much has been written about the reasons for their failure; the difficulty of changing an existing product portfolio, and the ability to grasp how quickly the market can turn its back on you, are clearly among the reasons. Experts in managerial thinking, cognition, and psychology, have argued that our deepest emotions affect our rationality. This suggests there is an individual and highly psychological aspect to how managers interpret and deal with business situations. On the other hand, we also know that entire organizations can have a particular mindset or culture. The innovative and hard-working spirit at Apple, the holistic and social orientation at Aravind and Natura, and the 'wolf' culture at Huawei, are all examples of this.

Below we will dig a little deeper into the psychology of management, in order to carve out what constitutes the mindset that modern managements are asked to have—those carrying the values of innovation, adaptability, creativity, and cooperation. What does the strategic mindset of tomorrow's capitalism and the emerging paradigm involve?

Strategy and Cognition

We begin with the smallest component: the human brain. Research is gradually revealing that our ideas of rational behavior, on which much of our modern society and capitalist structure is built, are naïve at best, and misleading.

Our rationality—what we believe to be a somehow neutral mechanism—is in fact a kind of deep cognitive hardwiring that is driven by the amygdala—the part of our brain that connects sensory stimulus with memory. When an individual receives any kind of external stimulus, the amygdala identifies it and searches the brain's memory bank to determine how to react to this stimulus. The core function of the amygdala is to ensure survival; therefore it is geared to assessing whether a situation or a person is dangerous or not. This happens within 80 milliseconds—faster than what can be consciously processed. There is no time for rational reflection on what type of action to take. This kind of reflection sets in later, but the deep emotion (fear or comfort, foe or friend) has already been identified and processed. All empirical activity is to some extent based on such emotional assessments with possible exceptions of strictly intellectual activity.

This corresponds with the research of Daniel Kahneman, one of the world's most influential psychologists and a Nobel laureate in economics, a truly defining figure in behavioral economics. Kahneman does not believe in economics as a rational regime, but rather explores the many human factors behind the theoretically rational models of the dominant macroeconomic elite. One of Kahneman's famous concepts is that of 'fast and slow thinking.' Fast thinking is what we do automatically without effort; slow thinking is when we do more complex tasks. Fast thinking corresponds with the quick emotional processing of the amygdala— useful for those fight-or-flight situations we needed to react to in early evolution. But the complex situations of modern life need slow thinking, not fast. Slow thinking instead demands a different kind of effort, where we use our logic, focus, and reflection to discern and shape our social and mental activity.[18]

That rational behavior does not drive this world is experientially obvious, yet the field of management has continued to create rational systems and models for strategic decisions over recent decades. Management as both theory and practice has built heavily on economic theory about markets, trade, and incentives. This is what people like Kahneman try to prove to be an idealistic rather than realistic representation of economics. The problem with economics and theoretically stringent models is that they ignore the human factor. Managers do not rationally calculate every single risk and opportunity in the market. Even if they did, the outcome would only be one interpretation of what is meant by that market, since the 'market' is not a neutral size that can be mathematically assessed. It is made by people. This is also why we observe bad managerial decisions: inside every individual manager is a complex cognitive system that assesses whether something is dangerous or safe.

Another powerful cognitive influence is how we experience rewards and punishments according to our actions and experience. When we succeed in something, we are rewarded by the release of dopamine in our brains—which makes us feel good. Financial gain has been found to be a high dopamine releaser, which can explain some of the short-sighted and greed-based decisions that we observe in parts of the corporate and financial worlds. If we follow this notion of hard-wired reward systems, how can we make the reward system of the brain match our emerging management values and not the short-sighted economic values of the industrial age?

First of all, we need to refine our understanding of what it means to gain value—to understand that hard financial value is not the one and only success factor out there. The issue is not just what releases dopamine in the corporate mind, but more how this mind is guided by the culture surrounding it. If 'gain' is also about obtaining the highest customer satisfaction rate in the company, this affects employees' and managers' behavior. If it means to be rated highly by internal peers as a great colleague and successful implementer, this drives motivation perhaps just as much as financial gain. Furthermore, motivation—and the rewards and reasoning structures of the brain—may be something much more sophisticated that these examples that are based on simplistic causality: *I do something right, people are happy, and then I get recognition and feel useful.*

Towards the end of this chapter we will consider how motivation can be much more that the mechanistic action-and-reward type. But first we will talk a little more about some of the cognitive traps that our brains make for us when we try to reason and enact the new values of management—those promoting innovation, adaptability, creativity, cooperation, and passion, and several other characteristics of our changing capitalist systems.

For many decades, neurologists have discussed the functions of the different parts of the brain, most importantly the lateralization between the two hemispheres of the brain—left and right. Many different hypotheses have been tested—among them that the left hemisphere deals with language and words, and the right hemisphere with images, or that the left hemisphere resembles masculine traits and the right hemisphere feminine traits. Over the years, much hemisphere analysis has become the domain of pop psychology, where various ideas of the rational vs. artistic sides of the brain flourish. As psychiatrist Iain McGilchrist notes in his seminal book on the divided brain, *The Master and His Emissary* (2009):

> These beliefs could, without much violence to the facts, be characterized as versions of the idea that the left hemisphere is somehow gritty, rational, realistic but dull, and the right hemisphere airy-fairy and impressionistic, but creative and exciting . . . In reality, both hemispheres are crucially involved in reason, just as they are in language; both hemispheres play their part in creativity. (p. 2)[19]

Serious neurological and psychiatric research has recognized that most *functions* of the brain take place in both the right and the left hemispheres, and the division is not clinically and theoretically poignant enough to indulge in further—at least it seems that the breadth of neuroscience today occupies itself with entirely other matters. But why then are there two halves to the brain? There must be some kind of division, exchange, and interaction between different abilities or capacities in our brains. One cue could be found in asking not what the brain hemispheres do, but *how* they do it. Research indicates that there are differences in this 'how': the left brain processes information more serially and in a singularly focused way, whereas the right brain does its processing more holistically and contextually. This has a bearing on how we understand the world at large—do we process it in bits or see the complex whole? The argument of scholars such as McGilchrist is that the Western culture has overrelied on the left-brain hemisphere in our pursuit of logics and reasoning for many centuries.

Put less dramatically, the left hemisphere does appear to have profound impact on our reasoning. It is a very strong ally in deducing and figuring out problems by focusing on their parts. But in today's increasingly interconnected world, where problems cannot be isolated and solved by focus and reason, but by flexibility, cooperation, and creativity, we need to bring the right brain into sharper focus. How we do this neurologically is a discussion beyond the scope

Unfortunately, too many managers unintentionally kill innovation because they rely too heavily on carrots and sticks to motivate employees . . . More than three decades of research have shown that people are most likely to be creative when they're intrinsically motivated by the interest, enjoyment, satisfaction, and challenge of the work itself.

(Teresa Amabile, Professor, Harvard Business School & Steve Kramer, psychologist and independent researcher. From the Harvard Business Review Blog, April 25, 2012)

of this book, but how we are socially and mentally able to train ourselves to use the right brain more, and in better ways, is another matter. By paying attention to the values and abilities we want to possess and express, we can change ourselves, our organizations and ultimately our larger social and economic structures too. Yes, there is a revolutionary flavor to this, but at the brink of a paradigm shift that matches the size of the transitions from feudal to industrial age some 140 years ago, we need to think as revolutionaries and believe that we can actually perform the required change in order to survive and stay fit.

Strategy, Different Mindsets, and Sets of Mind

In some of the examples and cases we have presented to this point, it is clear that the right and left brain can work together with much more balance and sophistication than traditional strategy advice dictates. One way of understanding the nature of organizational behavior is to look at the culture behind it—what we will call the *mindset* of the company.

Different research has tried to identify which kinds of mindsets are out there, and what type of mindset matches different organizations and commercial situations. This kind of research focuses on finding correlations between mindsets and organizational effects, and looks for contrasts between what the mindset is and what it is not. Some identified mindset types are for example:

- global vs. local mindset
- strategic vs. operational mindset
- innovation vs. routine mindset

But the challenges associated with this approach are tangible:

1. The dichotomist nature of thinking *either/or* in organizational foci does not fit the emerging paradigm of a *both/and* world. Here the local and the global are equally present and significant; long-term strategy must be combined with short-term execution; and innovation and creativity are not alternative new strategies but an imperative for continuous success.
2. The notion that you can analytically isolate certain mindsets does not correspond well with an empirical setting where organizational mindsets might not be so pure and easily discernible. It is a very theoretical way of dealing with the organizational mind, soon resulting in a mindset for every occasion; should management then strive to incorporate *several* mindsets in order to be both global and local, both strategic and operational, and so on?

The biggest challenge in the context of corporate strategy though, is to actually *create* the right mindset. Here, organizational mindset research is at an early embryonic stage. Other disciplines such as change management and organizational learning are trying to understand how organizations can change their habits and learn to think in new ways by looking at different levels, functions, and objectives of the organization. This is easily directed at top managers and can easily become the kind of cookbook scenario we have argued so strongly against. The naïve idea is that a senior leader has a vision, and then makes a plan for everyone else to understand and enact it, and even to change their cultural and cognitive behavior to fit the vision. This is not likely to happen, we argue, without the engagement and interaction of any company's most valuable resource: the employees (and other stakeholders, for that matter). However, today many companies are subscribing to the number-driven top-down approach followed by a hard-core execution plan. The implications are also that the strategy is not being well executed.[20]

Change and Motivation

Change comes in many forms. The traditional strategic management mode of changing the organization is often somewhat mechanistic and follows a plan. Top management sits down and identifies problems. It then identifies—perhaps with the help of a consultancy firm—how to meet these problems. This entails changes in the objectives, team efforts, and structures of the organization. If more radical, it also involves changing the minds and behaviors of employees (and managers). For example, management creates new processes that empower employees to take different and/or more responsibility, and it builds up (together with employees sometimes) a vision and mission for everyone to feel, follow, and enact. These are some of the new elements and they seem to support the focus on values, adaptability, and innovation of the emerging paradigm. But some of the examples we have presented thus far, and manifold others, are much more experimental in their change management approaches. Some are even radical.

Some companies are realizing that to stay ahead in the disruption game of the future, they need less compartmentalization and narrowly focused left-brain thinking and more holistic flexibility of the right brain. They need not just to make elaborate change management projects, but to create the conditions for change at a much more foundational level: the level of employees' ability to unleash their full creative and value-creating capacity. This demands a completely new starting point where each employee is motivated to—and supported in—making change happen continuously.

But the management practices around motivation are themselves tainted by our old industrial and mechanistic modes of organizing. As we know, motivation is often tied to bonuses and other economic incentives and generally to a performance/reward kind of culture. This is what author and business provoca-teur Daniel H. Pink calls Motivation 2.0.[21] The next level is Motivation 3.0, he argues. This is where managers and employees alike are valued for their intrinsic motivation and problem-solving abilities, rather than the need for financial or other extrinsic kinds of rewards. Here, management and control of employees' time and activity is scrapped, and instead companies experiment with approaches as radical as the ROWE system: the Results-Only Work Environment, in which work hours, office time, and whatever comes with the stress of clocking in and showing one's daily input is abandoned. Instead, employees work on projects and goals and have overarching deadlines to meet these. ROWE cases show increased productivity and reduced stress. Who would not embrace such a way of working?

But if employees are to be self-directive, they need to be as passionate about their jobs as is the entrepreneur who founds his own business. This goes for managers, too. Engagement is central. In traditional management, however, engagement is something that would just be *implemented* through, for example, a grand HR initiative launched with the promotion of top management—perhaps consisting of compensation schemes, team-building activities, nice stories on the intranet, and so on.

NOT *WHY* BUT *HOW* THE EMERGENCE TAKES PLACE

In this chapter we have not paid particular attention to *why* the conventional paradigm doesn't suffice—Chapters 1 and 2 have already paved the way for the discussion of an emerging new paradigm, radically different from the existing paradigm. Rather, we have focused on specific drivers.

One, as we have seen, is disruption. The new paradigm emerges on the back of radically increased levels of disruption and even companies based on 'disruptive-by-nature' strategies. Peaceful value creation is the hidden mantra of the conventional paradigm however; in reality disruptive business models and strategies are gaining momentum and strategy theory is therefore lagging behind practice to a considerable extent.

This is partly linked to the second cornerstone of this chapter, namely mind-set. Rumelt's 'smooth-sailing fallacy' is to the point here, because much of our strategic mindset is tainted by complacency, risk aversion, linear thinking, and business as usual. However, new landmarks in research tell us that the assump-tion of strict rationalism does not apply in a rapidly changing world, and that consequently we need to pay more attention to risk-taking, reverse thinking, and creativity.[22]

It would be appealing to conclude at this stage that the emerging paradigm is solely concerned with a 'creative disruption mindset.' However, the emerging paradigm is far more complex than that. To do it justice, we have devoted a separate chapter, Chapter 4, to uncover its broader scope.

KEY REFLECTIONS

A. Innovation is one of the keys to substantial change. Disruptive innovation is even more critical. Are you able to link disruptive innovation and a paradigm shift within strategy?

B. We are blind to our own blindness. We are tainted by the conventional paradigm which works within the known universe. We like to fool ourselves that there is a recipe for gold. We see what we want to see. This makes it easy for the black swan to swim under the radar. So how can we strengthen theory on strategy so that it addresses today's black swan realities?

C. The emerging paradigm is prompted by creative destruction, disruptive innovation, and the rejection of the conventional mindset. What else might drive the emerging new paradigm?

NOTES

1 See Schumpeter, Joseph (1942), *Capitalism, Socialism and Democracy*, Harper, New York.

2 See Christensen, Clayton M. (1997), *The Innovator's Dilemma: when new technologies cause great firms to fail*, Harvard Business School Press, Boston.

3 Tjan, Anthony K., Harrington, Richard J., and Hsieh, Tsun Yan (2012), *Heart, Smarts, Guts, and Luck*, Harvard Business Review Press, Boston (see in particular p. 202f.).

4 Ibid. p. 205.

5 In Hamel, Gary (2012), *What Matters Now: How to win in a world of relentless change, ferocious competition, and unstoppable innovation*, Jossey-Bass, New York (see also: http://blogs.wsj.com/management/2010/02/22/deconstructing-apple-part-i; Hamel's topics—values, innovation, adaptability, passion, and ideology—are addressed in the following sections).

6 Haque, Umair (2011), *The New Capitalist Manifesto—Building a disruptively better business*, Harvard Business Review Press, Boston.

7 Ibid. p. 15. Later on, Haque also galvanizes this by stating: "We're using rules built for hunting to manage an ark, but that approach to prosperity is past its sell-by date. The real crisis is bigger than banks, bonuses, or bailouts: it's that twentieth century institutions aren't fit for twenty-first-century economics" (p. 17).

8 Ibid. p. 29.

9 Based on the disruptors in: EIU (2008), *Global Disruptors: Steering through the storms* and EIU (2011), *The Long View: Getting new perspective on strategic risk* (London).

10 Taleb, Nassim Nicholas (2010), *The Black Swan: The impact of the highly improbable*, Random House, New York.

11 Ibid. See in particular his ch. 7 on non-linearity.

12 Hawkins, D.M. (1980), *Identification of Outliers*.

13 Paukku, Markus and Välikangas, Liisa, Outlier organizations and systematic transitions: Towards a research agenda, *Strategic Management Society*, 31st Conference, Prague, September 2012.

14 See Gifford, Jonathan (2012), *Blindsided: How business and society are shaped by our irrational and unpredictable behaviour,* Marshall Cavendish Business, London.

15 Ibid. p. 222f.

16 Greg Smith, Executive Director in Goldman Sachs: Why I am leaving Goldman Sachs (www.nytimes. com/2012/03/14/opinion/why-i-am-leaving-goldman-sachs.html?_r=1&pagewanted=all).

17 Rumelt, Richard (2012), *Good Strategy Bad Strategy: The difference and why it matters,* Profile Books, London, p. 289.

18 Kahneman, Daniel (2011), *Thinking Fast and Slow,* Allen Lane, New York.

19 See McGilchrist, Iain (2009), *The Master and His Emissary: The divided brain and the making of the Western World,* Yale University Press, New Haven, CT.

20 Roger, Martin (2010), The execution trap, *Harvard Business Review,* July.

21 Pink, Daniel (2010), *Drive: The surprising truth about what motivates us,* Canongate, London.

22 See also the inspiring article by Foss and Lindenberg (2013), Microfoundations for Strategy: A goal-framing perspective on the drivers of value creation, *Academy of Management Perspectives,* 27(2), 85–102, in particular on an oblique approach and transformational leadership.

Chapter 4

Towards a New Paradigm?

A TIME OF TRANSITION

We saw in the last chapter that disruptive innovation and a changed mindset can be key drivers towards an emerging new paradigm in strategy and management. In the preceding chapters we addressed some of the deficiencies in conventional literature and research.

Rather systematically outliers have been treated as bad data points. Because they make arriving at a comfortable mean or average too troublesome, the lazy solution has often been to ignore outliers. But a general regression to the mean leads to the adoption of common practices, like the recipes in the cookbook literature or convergence on best (common) practice. The implication of this has been decades of homogenization of management and strategy within companies, allowing for systematic generalizations and ignorance towards heterogeneity.

This recipe-based paradigm of homogenization is being increasingly challenged for several good reasons. First, as we have shown in earlier chapters, the recipe universe is based on uncomfortable preconditions and assumptions, with the result that many recipes do not deliver on their promises. Second, and in line with the increasingly homogeneous structure of the conventional paradigm, companies and entire industries have become increasingly vulnerable to outliers, disruptive innovations, unknowns, and, not least, black swans. Third, the growing success of black swans implies that we need a new paradigm which is more in keeping with the heterogeneous black swans than the homogeneous failures of the conventional paradigm.

In this chapter we will address the substance of such an emerging new paradigm. First of all, we will pick out the fact that some of the more recent literature demonstrates that a paradigm shift is now quickly gaining momentum. Gary Hamel's *What Matters Now* provides a good illustration of this process. Hamel's tendency to look for and present a recipe definitely belongs to the conventional paradigm. Yet some of his thinking suggests the emergence of a new paradigm.[1]

A more straightforward example which illustrates the new paradigm is Vijay Govindarajan and Chris Trimble's *Reverse Innovation*.[2] The authors reverse the existing thinking that innovation should take place close to home, and in rich developed countries. The global dynamics of innovation is changing so much that innovation in the future will flow in the reverse direction, namely from the developing countries to developed ones. A good example of this, which is drawn on in the book, is that of GE which managed to disrupt itself in Asia.

We argue however that there is an urgent need for a *complete* shift towards a new paradigm. The case for this has already been addressed—i.e. that the existing recipes are inadequate, and that experience shows that many companies are actually *worse off* using these standardized and homogeneous recipes than not using them. In this context, we maintain that the conventional normative approach to promise top managers guaranteed success is now quickly approaching the end of its life cycle.

Moreover, our research on black swan companies demonstrates that there is a growing gap between the prescriptions of the conventional literature and the actual course of action taken by these successful market disrupters.

With this in mind, we will now set out some of the key dimensions of what we see as an emerging new paradigm. To allow comparisons, we have chosen to address the same dimensions as dealt with in the analysis of the conventional paradigm. These are:

1. The surprise dimension.
2. The innovation dimension.
3. The cost dimension.
4. The X-factor dimension.
5. The regulatory dimension.

We will address each of these in turn.

FIVE IMPORTANT DIMENSIONS OF THE EMERGING PARADIGM

The Surprise Dimension

In the conventional paradigm, market leadership is crucial to success.[3] In what we term the emerging paradigm the perfect starting position is to possess a market share equal to zero. Michael Porter and others share this enthusiasm for companies acting as first movers, the rationale being that they can quickly grab the lion's share of a given market. In the conventional paradigm being the first mover is a special asset and, according to Porter, a very important tool to achieve competitive advantage. But it shouldn't be forgotten that being first can come at a price; that is, it cannot be assumed that this will automatically lead to success and maximum profit.

In the emerging paradigm it is a greater advantage to be the *last* mover or, better still, an unexpected mover. With Apple, this has been manifest in its 'surprise' tactics around the invention and unveiling of the iPhone. It was a deliberate move on Apple's part to keep its activities tightly under wraps, so that no one outside the company knew what it was up to—maximizing the market impact, and minimizing rivals' ability to prepare a counter move. At Chinese telecommunications equipment vendor Huawei, it was the unprecedented growth realized by its strategy of countryside surrounding cities, rather than technological leapfrogging, that took the market by surprise. At Aravind, the Indian eye hospital, combining established cataract surgery technology with a McDonald-like assembly-line process was the key to success, enabling unprecedented high productivity at a very low unit cost, something no one else could match because the idea had never occurred to them. In the airline industry, late mover Emirates has now emerged as the world's second largest carrier, challenging the number one position, with Dubai as a strategic hub geographically. Few, if any, of these moves could have been predicted. Each of these players threw the competition a curve ball.

Elsewhere, Latin American cosmetic company Natura is now bursting onto the scene with a new kind of globalized beauty strategy, based not just on outer but also inner beauty. Indian underdog conglomerate Tata, meanwhile, has challenged the legacy of British colonialism with its swift, unforeseen acquisitions of some major, iconic British brands.

The common denominator uniting all of these cases is that no one expected these moves—with the result that no effective response was ever prepared by these companies' peers. This is why black swans are so dangerous—their arrival is not expected, so no one is watching for them. This gives them maximum opportunity to perfect their offering and take the market by surprise.

The newer the company, or the less of an existing investment it has in a particular market, the less encumbered they are by legacy behavior or traditional thinking. Being the 'new kid on the block' usually means a company is able to shun prevailing market irrationalities and accepted ways of doing things, leaving them free to experiment and go off at their own tangent.

The differing mindsets of black swans versus market incumbents are also a significant contributor, of course. When a company or its management pursues a recipe for success—based on the assumption that they live in a homogeneous, predictable environment—they are fixing their mindset on a reality that no longer exists. As well as ensuring that the company misses new opportunities, because it can't imagine them, this increases the opportunity for the black swan waiting in the reeds. Its attack will be all the sweeter, and its impact on the market so much the greater, because no one saw it coming. While traditional market players are continuing to do things one way, the black swan is ready to blow them out of the water with its disruptive reverse-thinking.

Consider the extent to which the importance of value creation has been drummed into managers over the last couple of decades. The trouble is that in making value *creation* such a core focus, managers (and their advisers) have overlooked the impact of value *destruction*, de-monetization of traditional revenue streams and the need for alternative revenue streams—for example if a black swan suddenly swooped into their market.

Some of the literature on disruption and discount business strategy addresses the notion of destruction.[4]

Just like some of the companies pursuing an aggressive discount business strategy, black swans often create massive value destruction, not least for the market incumbents. While others are focusing on slowly developing their value creation, black swans can suddenly create value *destruction* in addition to the value that they create for themselves. This is highlighted by the impact on Nokia of Apple entering the mobile phone market with the iPhone. This seismic event did as much to destroy Nokia's hold on the market as it did to propel Apple to a strong new position.

Similarly Huawei, Tata, and Natura are radically challenging the value in their respective industries, in these cases from a base in emerging economies. The airline and eye surgery examples cited previously provide further evidence that traditional players in all sorts of markets cannot afford to be complacent.

All of the black swan companies mentioned have entered swiftly and potentially catastrophically for the white swans that were preoccupied with preening themselves and feeling superior. Black swans have no time for vanity, nor do they buy into the notion of competitive advantage. Rather than following the conventional paradigm as articulated by Michael Porter, black swans swim to their own tune—a new emerging paradigm.

McGrath sums up the situation like this:

> Strategy is stuck. For too long the business world has been obsessed with the notion of building a sustainable competitive advantage. That idea is at the core of most strategy textbooks . . . In a world where a competitive advantage often evaporates in less than a year, companies can't afford to spend months at a time crafting a single long-term strategy. To stay ahead, they need to constantly start new strategic initiatives, building and exploiting many *transient competitive advantages* at once.[5]

Despite the fact that McGrath uses other case examples than those we have chosen—she draws on Milliken & Company, a US-based textiles and chemicals company; Cognizant, a global IT service company; and Brambles, a logistics company based in Australia—she too analyzes companies that have rejected the inherent assumption that stability in business is the norm.

Our black swans operate on the basis of continuous change, and a need to be agile—to the extent that the surprise factor can be utilized as a tactical weapon, destroying existing value while simultaneously creating substantial new value for themselves and their customers.

Given that black swans are moving in this way, the emerging paradigm must as a minimum allow room for the following notions:

- *zero market share could provide the optimum starting point* (as opposed to market *leadership* based on competitive advantage under the conventional paradigm); and
- *to be late or even last to market, or to enter left field as an unexpected mover,* is preferable to the idea of first-mover advantage as set out in the conventional paradigm.

The Innovation Dimension

Conventional innovation is very often based on a Michael Porter-*esque* strategy of differentiation. In Porter's universe, this advantage would flow from development of the additional value that a company is able to create (read: innovate) thereby differentiating itself from its peers. Usually this would involve looking at other companies and doing something different, or the same thing differently.

Under the emerging paradigm, companies like Huawei, Apple, Emirates, Ryanair, Aravind, Google, Amazon, and Tata are examples of companies thinking out of the box—not only in the way they innovate, but also in the extent to which they *disrupt*, thereby setting a new standard. The new standard represents a view where the companies are not only looking at their *own* value creation (which, after all, would often be part of the existing paradigm) but likewise on *impact* tactics—i.e. the disruption of competitors.

Such companies are not looking at best practice (which is irrelevant because it is based on the market leadership of incumbents) but at 'next practice' or 'future practice.' The case of General Electric, as described in *How GE Is Disrupting Itself,*[6] is very illuminating in this context.

The starting point for GE was to take the unprecedented leap of innovating substantially far from home, in the process creating a new practice of 'reverse innovation.' Rather than simply continuing to innovate in its home country of the US, GE chose to begin with a clean slate and see what it could achieve in China and India. This is a rare and impressive behavior for such a well-established company with such a long history.

Our primary foci are not on incumbents however, but rather on black swan companies. Although some such organizations employ similar tactics, they do so in a more revolutionary and unexpected context. Take again the case of Apple whose highly disruptive assault on the market with the iPhone was orchestrated by a single individual—Steve Jobs. With this groundbreaking product, Apple managed to create a new ecosystem crossing traditional industries including music, mobility, internet, broadband, third-party applications, and more. Focusing its innovation efforts in Cupertino in the US, Apple quickly emerged as the world's largest company. Its behavior was not as out of character as that of GE in that Apple did not feel the need to go abroad to break out of its mold, yet Apple surpassed GE by quite some distance in terms of commercial success. Its boldness was more about diversifying the 'I'-concept into other business streams.

The case of Tata is different again. Given its Indian heritage background it might have been expected that the group would focus its innovation energies on its own emerging market. Yet as can be seen from the conglomerate's highly successful entry into the automotive sector, Tata had surprise tactics up its sleeve. It decided to develop its high-end cars in the UK, by 'imperializing' one of the former British crown jewels, Jaguar Land Rover. This gave it speed to market and, being an unexpected move, had massive impact. So could this represent the beginning of a new wave of left-field innovation, whereby companies in the BRIC countries are able to leapfrog their competitors at innovation by swallowing up troubled businesses in industrially developed countries?

Another interesting case is the Chinese company, Huawei. In contrast to Tata, it has focused its innovation in its domestic market where it has quickly established one of the world's largest portfolios of patents. As a late mover in its chosen field, the company had an advantage over its modern-day peers in that it was able to adopt IP-based technologies from the start of its growth story and its subsequent emergence as a black swan. It is no coincidence that Huawei's growth rate has already passed most of the incumbent players in its target industry. The company seemingly came from nowhere, but, not held back by legacy investments, was able to enter right at the heart of the current action.

While each of these examples is different, together they show that it is possible to innovate substantially and with a huge impact if unprecedented leaps are taken. None of the companies described above subscribed to known best practice in setting out their strategies. Rather they established their own proprietary practice, something we have termed '*next* practice.'

Natura is the best example yet of next practice, something the company has exhibited from the outset. Its revolutionary approach in its chosen market has been to combine inner and external health and beauty, and to employ an unprecedented crowd-based sales strategy.

Emirates, the airline, has been similarly ambitious. It had the audacity to take on long-established approaches to air travel, challenging global travel trajectories and turning route planning upside down by proposing a new global air network with Dubai as the central hub. At a technological level, meanwhile, the company has defined next practice with a young fleet and heavy investments in fuel reduction.

Summarizing, the emerging paradigm reflects the following traits:

■ *Substantial innovation paired with disruptive impact tactics* (as opposed to piecemeal differentiation based on value creation).
■ *Revolutionary and unprecedented leaps* (compared with the marginal, incremental, or evolutionary character of the conventional paradigm).
■ *Next practice or future practice* (rather than the retrospectively defined best practice of the conventional paradigm).

Moreover, a striking trait of the innovation dimension is that black swans often innovate based on *passion*, which calls for the *heart* attribute laid out by Tjan et al.[7] Certainly entrepreneurs are much more likely to be motivated and driven by passion than by the very analytical methodology expounded by the conventional paradigm.

Having looked at how black swans take markets by surprise and fare very differently in the innovation dimension, we will now consider how such companies also challenge our understanding of cost.

The Cost Dimension

A new type of company has emerged that does not charge customers, apparently offering customers products and services for free, or almost for free. Take for example discount airlines such as Ryanair, search engines like Google, and IP-based telecoms services like Skype.

In his book, *Free: The Future of a Radical Price*, Chris Anderson lays out the various business models behind this phenomenon. Interestingly, he also explains in some depth how Google, Wikipedia, Ryanair, and many other modern-day market challengers *'de-monetize'* existing businesses. He concludes however that this is no bad thing:

> In each case the winners far outnumber the losers. Free is disruptive,
> to be sure, but it tends to leave more efficient markets in its wake.
> The trick is to ensure you've bet on the winning side.[8]

Conventional cost models are still based on the old school of microeconomics, which asserts that it is vital to the success of a business that it can cover average costs. Yet some of the black swans pursuing the Free model have been hugely profitable—often more so than the existing market leaders, as has been seen in the example of Ryanair. Generally, this is because companies following a Free model gain revenues from alternative sources, for example by charging for additional services (as is the case with Ryanair, Aravind, and Skype), or through partnerships with third parties and reverse revenue streams (as happens with Google). Price elasticity allows these companies to attract far more customers than if they had followed traditional pricing models. Through volume, or economies of scale, they are then able to bring average costs down considerably.

Companies fuelling the emerging paradigm introduce cost structures that the existing incumbents cannot match or think are unrealistic. The model that those including Ryanair, Skype, Google, Amazon, Aravind, Emirates, Tata, Huawei, South West Airlines, and many others have successfully adopted are simple enough. Each of these companies has achieved success by delivering a good service at a surprisingly low price. Importantly, this low customer pricing goes hand in hand with even lower underlying costs, resulting in a profit—something traditional players may be struggling to achieve.

A notable exception to this rule is Apple, whose approach to pricing bucks the trend. Apple is not the strongest in its industry in terms of unit shipments; at the time of writing it is the strongest in terms of revenues and margin however, ensuring high profitability. This in turn has had a significant impact on Apple's market capitalization which was the world's highest in 2011–2013. Just because the iPhone has been priced at a premium from the very beginning does not mean that the underlying costs of the company are high. In fact, being a very late mover in the mobile handset market, Apple has managed to produce its smartphones at a much lower price than some of its peers, including Nokia who is still struggling to get a foothold in the smartphone market.

The cost base of eye-care specialist Aravind is interesting, too; it is successfully undercutting traditional competitors with a unit price of USD 18 compared with USD 1800 for companies working in the context of conventional thinking. Similarly health and beauty specialist Natura is much more profitable than its peers despite much lower retail prices. In both cases, this success is down to disruptively low cost bases.

Also Huawei has its own approach to costs. It boasts an unmatched cost structure based on lowest Chinese production costs and attractive state-financed credit facilities for certain customers. In some cases this allows for a kind of 'pay as you grow' business model, whereby customers settle their bills for infrastructure bought from Huawei after they have reached positive cash flows from their operations. Until repayment commences, this model may also be characterized as a new subset of the free paradigm, in that the cost of the infrastructure delivered is not always recouped by Huawei at the time of delivery.

In summary, the cost dimension is barely addressed in the conventional paradigm, which invokes traditional rules from microeconomics such as pricing based on average costs. Black swans, by contrast, employ a *disruptive cost structure*, allowing the alignment of cost and price elasticity.[9]

The X-Factor Dimension

According to the conventional paradigm, it is important to plan thoroughly and to get this absolutely right. Prevailing strategy thinking advocates that companies should opt for a strategy process with analytic elements and harnessing well-known models (such as Five Forces, SWOT, VRIO, 7 S, and Strategic Canvas), arriving at a manual-like format which is agreed by (or at least known to) salient parts of the organization.

Within the emerging paradigm, such a traditional strategy process makes little or no sense. The emerging paradigm takes as its point of departure the contention that the rational assumptions underpinning the conventional paradigm do not stand up to scrutiny. Phil Rosenzweig notes that much business thinking is tainted by errors of logic and flawed judgments that distort a proper understanding of the real reasons for a company's performance. His book, *The Halo Effect . . . and the Eight Other Business Delusions That Deceive Managers*, presents ample evidence of the pitfalls of relying on the assumption that a diligently worked out business strategy, on the basis of strict rational components, will lead to success.[10]

By contrast there is plenty of empirical evidence, especially recently, of companies eliciting a high Return on Strategy in unplanned, unexpected, or seemingly irrational circumstances (when measured against the common understanding of what makes sense). Chris Anderson[11] was probably the first to explore the concept of 'free' services in any detail, explaining how the companies cited earlier could achieve so much by offering core products and services without charge—a market proposition that would not make (rational) sense under the conventional paradigm.

Meanwhile Mullins and Komisar brilliantly made the point that if companies

According to Rosenzweig, the wise manager understands that:

- Any good strategy involves risk. If you think your strategy is foolproof, the only fool is likely to be you.
- Execution, too, is uncertain—what works in one company with one workforce may have different results elsewhere.
- Chance often plays a greater role than we think, or than successful managers usually like to admit.
- The link between inputs and outcomes is tenuous. Bad outcomes don't always mean that managers have made mistakes; and good outcomes don't always mean they have acted astutely.

But when the die is cast, the best managers act as if chance is irrelevant; persistence and tenacity are everything.

stick to their first strategy plan (Plan A or the conventional paradigm) very often they will not succeed. Their work, *Getting to Plan B. Breaking through to a Better Business Model*,[12] sets out some important steps towards better and more realistic business models. Crucially, Mullins' and Komisar's book presents strategy as something that cannot be finite. Rather, it must be viewed as a mental framework where smart strategic changes can be made with immediacy, and the strategic course corrected before it is too late.

When a traditional plan has reached its limits, and the need for something less formalized, less rational, and less foreseen becomes evident, what is the key to an alternative, more relevant, and effective strategy?

This is where the elusive 'X' factor comes into play—that hard-to-define element that sets disruptive black swan companies apart from their traditional white swan peers. This unknown quantity is something the conventional paradigm does not allow for. The X factor is not something that can be entered into a mathematical equation. Rather, it has been defined as:

> A critical but undefinable element. Also a noteworthy special talent or quality.[13]

Steve Wozniak, former CEO of Apple, has said the following about defining moments in Apple's history:

> All the best things that I did at Apple came from (a) not having money and (b) not having done it before, ever.[14]

The X factor, then, is something that cannot be put into a conventional context. The normal textbook understanding of the path to success—in which the X factor does not exist or is neglected—is based on the availability of comfortable funding for a project, and relies heavily on experience. In the context of black swans, it is the X factor that takes center stage. In Chapters 5–12, we will see that all black swans are united in their active exploitation of their respective X factors, allowing them to maximize their Return on Strategy.

How black swan companies actively work with the X factor, or the degree to which they are dependent on its existence, varies considerably however. In the case of Apple, it was embodied in the talents of Steve Jobs and his way of meeting as yet unknown demands innovatively, with a reverse methodology. As we will explore later in the book, Steve Jobs was able to both make unknowns known, and—through internal security measures and his own personal stewardship—keep *knowns* unknown!

For eye-care specialist Aravind, the X factor is tied to the innovative way the company has managed to slash the cost of eye surgery by a factor of 100—through the use of eye 'camps' and on-the-spot surgery and by harnessing cheaper, cutting-edge lenses. In principle, this model could be applied almost anywhere else in the world, not just in India.

Emirates' success, on the other hand, is directly linked to its location. Dubai creates the backdrop for the airline and Emirates creates the background for Dubai; the two are therefore inextricably linked in a kind of 'chicken-and-egg' relationship.

Huawei's X factor is tied to its core strategy—of targeting the countryside surrounding cities. By identifying and targeting this specific market, it too was able to launch a black swan attack on its industry. There are some similarities with Aravind, which initially gained traction in rural areas, to arrive at costs which are unthinkable elsewhere.

The X factor may also be embodied in a single person. This is the case at Ryanair whose CEO, Michael O'Leary, has long been preoccupied with a business model based on disruption. Not only that, but he has also allowed his own personality to shape the communication processes around the execution of his plans, becoming the personification of the airline's X factor.

Tata is different again. Based in an emerging, not very industrially developed country, the group has successfully managed to take over a number of iconic brands in developed countries, making some of these further profitable by satisfying undiscovered demand in emerging countries. Following its acquisition of British car manufacturer Jaguar Land Rover, more Land Rovers have been sold in China than in the UK.

In a nutshell, the conventional paradigm is based on everything being planned to the nth degree, and everything being explainable, but as we have seen, Plan A rarely plays out, everything is uncertain and risks are high. It is in this vacuum that theory and practice leave room for the X factor to operate. Black swans succeed because they take full advantage of the X factor, including *the unexplained, the unplanned, and the unexpected.*

Before we look more closely at the inner workings of black swans, let us first examine the regulatory dimension which is too often overlooked.

The Regulatory Dimension

In a more conventional context, regulation is not part of the business strategy toolkit. Regulation is considered to be fair and impartial, helped by the fact that market participants are competing in a known and level playing field.

Empirical evidence suggests that, with the odd exception, the opposite is true. Consider the following:

■ How would Chinese telecom equipment provider Huawei fare without subsidies, low-interest loans, generous export credits, a large home market on a semi-exclusive basis for a number of years, a governmental helping hand in Africa, etc.?

- Would the American car manufacturing industry have survived without governmental bail-out assistance?
- In a considerable number of countries, banks are not allowed to go bankrupt. Would such banks be able to survive if there were no governmental support?
- In some industries—such as pharmaceuticals—regulatory approvals are necessary in order to launch medical products in a country. The FDA in the US has achieved international status for food and drug approvals. These as important as competition between companies?
- Does government support in the form of huge subsidies come out of the blue?

Regulatory distortions, regulatory forbearance, regulatory capture, diverse subsidies, and non-regulation together form a cocktail of possibilities and threats to companies. The impact on their business execution is considerable, albeit often unpredictable in form, character, strength, etc.

For companies to effectively disrupt, they also need to understand their external environment.

One of the most important factors with significant impact on business opportunities is the regulatory structure and environment, which governs corporate behavior. Regulation is a tangible economic factor, and large corporations dedicate substantial resources to dealing with its effects and influencing its development. Companies can do several things in response to regulatory developments, of which we will address the following:

1. The fact that companies can *influence* regulation towards creating conditions that are more favorable from a corporate or industry perspective.
2. The fact that companies can *use* regulation to identify new business potential.

For half a century, corporations have excelled in the first of these two, i.e. influencing regulations. Since the late 1960s, which saw an upturn in civil interest groups and government regulation in areas such as health, environment, and working conditions, companies have invested heavily to advocate their interests.[15] Pan-industry associations such as the US Chamber of Commerce in the US serve companies across the country with extensive Washington lobbying, and engage in political opinion making, not least through supporting favored political candidates at state and federal levels. Public relation firms and law firms are other strategic tools for creating, shaping, or changing public policy and regulation. And most large companies themselves staff large public affairs units, dedicated to understanding regulatory developments and lobbying their interests in federal and state politics. This trend is also seen in other geographies. By 2012, more than 5,000 interest groups had registered with the EU's Transparency Register of which more than 700 are individual companies and corporations. Added to these are the numerous consultancy firms which companies engage for specific matters, and trade associations. Many more have not registered but exercise their influence through various networks and personal associations.

Though this engagement with and influence over regulation is common, strategy research does not tend to concern itself much with this. Government affairs, public affairs, and public relations are references that come up very rarely among strategy scholars. In four of the top journals in management and organization, these concepts have been thematized fewer than ten times in total since the 1980s![16]

The second response to regulation—to use it as a means for new business development—seems even less developed in strategy research, though there is a strong place for it. This need comes first of all because rapid changes in business and financial development bring with them changes in regulations. As we showed in Chapter 3, corporate scandals in the early 2000s resulted in substantial law packages such as the Sarbanes–Oxley Act, and the financial breakdown of 2007/2008 caused the set of restrictive laws that we know from the Dodd–Frank Wall Street Reform and Consumer Protection Act of 2010. Operating in global markets forces companies' need to adjust to other national regulations as well as their own. This may favor existing national businesses, and/or may incorporate policy areas to which the company has not yet had to conform (for example, environmental protection laws); certainly they may be difficult to comprehend, and expensive to respond to. Third, global markets are changing; BRIC country economies are soaring against the traditionally power-wielding Western economies. This affects global and bilateral trade agreements, changes consumer patterns, and creates new global brands with a home base in emerging markets, etc.

Western corporations perceive this as an ever-greater challenge. The Economist Intelligence Unit, based on a survey of corporate executives, ranks global policy issues as the third biggest concern of companies. More precisely it is the "increased complexity of operating in multiple social, political, and regulatory environments," which corporate executives see as a powerful influencer on their existing and future business.[17]

When it comes to the two overarching approaches to regulatory developments, practical developments are far ahead of what strategy theory and research can offer. This means that when we talk about corporate strategy and the external environment of companies, we more or less ignore the influence of the state and other public domains, as well as the strategic opportunities that may arise in regulatory developments. It also means that the strategic management scholarly field neglects to help companies with tools and analyses to tackle the increasingly complex regulatory demands they face. In terms of both of these agendas—opportunity and demand—the regulatory dimension presents high potential for black swan strategies.

As will become evident from subsequent chapters, addressing the regulatory dimension has been a key component of Huawei's approach to market disruption. To take one example, the company has often been more or less part of interstate agreements between the Chinese government and governments of developing countries. It has also received a helping hand from the Chinese government in terms of credit facilities and, initially certainly, easy access to a large home market.

At Aravind, the regulatory dimension is tied to working with NGOs, researchers, and governmental offices to enhance efficiency and achieve quality of service/ products. Essentially, Aravind carries out functions which in a number of countries are considered part of public welfare programs.

Ryanair, as an airline, clearly operates within a regulated environment. Yet this doesn't necessarily mean that the company shouldn't try to expand or change the rules and regulations—as difficult as this might be. For example, Ryanair has for years tried to acquire the formerly state-owned Irish airline, Aer Lingus. However, each time it has put in a bid for the company, both the Irish authorities and the EU Commission have reacted negatively, arguing that the merger would kill the competition and undermine consumer choice. In a second example, Ryanair has been trying to develop a 'standing' option—vertical seating—on flights for some years now—a considerable challenge in a very conservative-thinking industry where passengers have always had to be seated during take-off and landing. Ryanair's willingness to challenge accepted norms is indicative of its disruptive approach to its market.

In summary, the regulatory dimension is important to all black swans—not least because this important dimension is often somewhat overlooked by their peers. This paves the way for black swans to extract further value for themselves and their customers, by working with the regulatory dimension and, as opportunities dictate, enjoying the Wild West status of this environment where there is an advantage in doing so.

The ensuing chapters will further touch on the regulatory dimension, however at this stage the interest in the topic of the emerging paradigm concerns the following:

■ *Regulatory distortions/wins*—considerable advantages and disadvantages are gained by companies depending on their success in the regulatory dimension. This will be further illustrated with reference to Huawei (Chapter 8) and Ryanair (Chapter 11). Conventional theory on strategy and management is of little help here as these matters are left to the market forces.

■ *Regulatory game changing* is either only marginally addressed or neglected in the conventional paradigm. Some regulatory institutions exercise regulatory forbearance to the advantage or disadvantage of the regulated companies. Again, Huawei with its strong ties to the Chinese government provides an example (see Chapter 8).

■ *National subsidies, home market preference, or cultural advantages* are a more direct way by which companies may gain advantages or disadvantages which apply to almost all of the companies addressed in Chapters 5–12. Emirates offers a potential example with its Dubai focus and UAE status (see Chapter 7).

FURTHER PERSPECTIVES

Addressing regulatory issues is of growing importance in a world populated by increasing numbers of black swans. At an MBA level in business schools this dimension is often missing and it is really only during the recent decade that matters related to corporate social responsibility have been a topic of some focus. However, in the emerging paradigm, regulatory issues will have an important place and become an increased focal point in the public affairs departments of companies.

The five dimensions depicted do not purport to be exhaustive. Rather, they offer some useful insight as we attempt to analyze and identify the character of what we have termed the emerging paradigm.

SUMMARIZING

An attempt to summarize the nature of, and differences between, the conventional and emerging paradigm is presented in Table 4.1.

In Chapters 5–12, we will delve deeper into the inner workings of a diverse selection of black swan companies to assess their relevance as regards the emerging paradigm. We will be drawing on examples already mentioned (as listed below), but looking at each in greater detail.

Chapter 5:   Apple
Chapter 6:   Aravind
Chapter 7:   Emirates
Chapter 8:   Huawei
Chapter 9:   Natura
Chapter 10:   Nokia (although not a black swan!)
Chapter 11:   Ryanair
Chapter 12:   Tata

Table 4.1
The Essence of the Emerging Paradigm Summarized

	Paradigm/ Terminology	Conventional Paradigm	Emerging Paradigm
The surprise dimension	Market position	Market leadership	Zero market share = perfect start
The surprise dimension	Starting block	First mover, pole position, and sustainable advantages	Late or last or unexpected mover and ephemeral advantages
The innovation dimension	Change mode	Differentiate and value creation	Innovate substantially and impact tactics
The innovation dimension	Size of change	Marginal/ incremental	Revolutionary, unprecedented leaps
The innovation dimension	Benchmarking technology	Best practice	Next practice
The innovation dimension	Methodology	Analytical	Passionate
The cost dimension	Cost structure	Conventional cost structure	Disruptive cost structure
The X-factor dimension	Degree of rationalization	Everything explained/planned	Focus on exploitation of the X dimension (the unexplained, the unplanned, the unexpected)
The regulatory dimension	Market perfection	Market forces	Regulatory distortions/ wins
The regulatory dimension	Regulatory forbearance	Marginally or not addressed	Regulatory game changing
The regulatory dimension	Governmental support	Marginally or not addressed	National subsidies, home market, or cultural advantages

KEY REFLECTIONS

A. The emerging new paradigm is upside down compared with the conventional paradigm. This means that a new vocabulary comes to light under five dimensions: surprise, innovation, cost, X factor, and regulation.

B. The five dimensions and the new underlying terminology provide a further indicator of the way to the new paradigm in continuation of the work of some renowned existing scholars who are already beginning to deviate from the conventional paradigm. These include Clayton Christensen, Gary Hamel, Vijay Govindarajan, and others.

C. The new paradigm is also crucial if we are to fully comprehend the ingenuity of the storytelling of the black swan companies developed in Part II of this book.

NOTES

1 Hamel, Gary (2012), *What Matters Now? How to win in a world of relentless change, ferocious competition, and unstoppable innovation,* Jossey-Bass, New York, disregarding the tendency to create a recipe which belongs to the conventional paradigm.

2 Govindarajan, Vijay and Trimble, Chris (2012), *Reverse Innovation: Create far from home win everywhere,* Harvard Business Review Press, Boston, not least the 'reverse thinking' which inhibits the notion of 'reverse innovation.'

3 See the notion of 'Competitive Advantage' based on Michael Porter's studies (Porter, M.E. (1980), *Competitive Advantage: Creating and sustaining superior performance,* Free Press, New York) and also the underlying PIMP-studies all stressing the importance of market leadership and first-mover advantages.

4 See Andersen and Poulfelt (2006), *Discount Business Strategy: How the new market leaders are redefining business strategy,* Wiley, New York.

5 McGrath, Rita Gunther (2013), *The End of Competitive Advantage* (the quote is taken from http.//hbr.org/2013/06/transient-advantage).

6 Govindarajan, Vijay and Trimble, Chris (October 2009), How GE is disrupting itself, *Harvard Business Review,* 56–65.

7 Tjan et al. (2012), *Heart, Smarts, Guts, and Luck.* Notwithstanding the fact that the authors are keen to treat all four attributes on an equal footing it seems as if "heart" has some preference when addressing innovation by entrepreneurs.

8 Anderson, Chris (2009), *Free: The Future of a Radical Price,* Hyperion, London, p. 131.

9 Ibid. See also Andersen and Poulfelt (2006), *Discount Business Strategy,* in which book the inner workings of some of the aggressive discount companies is addressed, and to a considerable extent discount equals disruption, see among others, p. 32f.

10 Rosenzweig, Phil (2007), *The Halo Effect.* The box corresponds to Rosenzweig's indents at p. 174.

11 Interestingly, Chris Anderson (see n. 8) is not a theorist.

12 Mullins, John and Komisar, Randy (2009), *Getting to Plan B: Breaking through to a Better Business Model,* Harvard Business Press, Boston. We are making reference to their findings that start-up processes are largely driven by poorly conceived business plans based on untested assumptions and serious flaws and irrationalities. We are not making reference to their own suggested approach which to some extent resembles a recipe.

13 Andersen, Froholt, and Poulfelt (2010), *Return on Strategy,* p. 9.

14 Ibid. p. 70.

15 See Barley, Steve (2010), Building an Institutional Field to Corral a Government, *Organization Studies,* 31(06).

16 Ibid.

17 See EIU (2008), *Global Disruptors: Steering through the storms* (London).

Part II

On the Inner Workings of Black Swans

Chapter 5

Apple, the Black Swan

A CYCLICAL BLACK SWAN?

Apple's rollercoaster history to date should be enough to caution any onlooker drawing conclusions about the company's successes. A closer look reveals a cyclical development to Apple's corporate performance. This should be taken into account particularly when tempted to assume that the company has 'made it', having seemingly achieved the pinnacle of success as suggested by its current all-time high.

As shown in Figure 5.1, Apple today holds by far the highest market capitalization among its peers (and indeed among all companies), according to 2012 figures.

One of the explanations is Apple's stronghold in the smartphone market. As highlighted in Figure 5.2, Apple is not actually the market leader in terms of shipments. However, in terms of value (measured by revenue), Apple stood out as a clear winner in 2012.

Interestingly, Apple's outperformance of its peers comes on the back of a much narrower product portfolio than can be seen with other companies in the industry.

	Mcap ($bn)
Samsung	215,8
Apple	506,8
Nokia	13,5
Sony	9,9
HTC	8,1
LGE	11,5
Lenovo	9,6
ZTE	4,7
RIM	6,3

FIGURE 5.1 Apple's Overall Market Capitalization, December 2012[1]

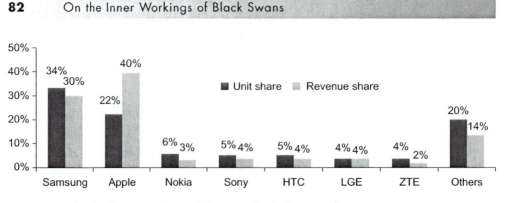

FIGURE 5.2 Apple, Strongest Not in Shipments But in Revenues[2]

For our purposes here, the idea is not to focus on Apple's corporate success or general performance, far less to attempt to provide a comprehensive view of the company. The intention is rather to highlight a few significant deviations from conventional thinking, with a view to more deeply exploring a couple of emerging paradigm components and black swan traits. Whereas external observers might see only the highly manifest beauty of Apple, we will concentrate our focus on some very specific inner workings of Apple which help explain the company's emergence as a black swan, most obviously surrounding the iPhone and related activities.

THE IMPORTANCE OF SECRECY OR THE PRINCIPLE OF 'SCARED SILENT'

A deeper analysis of Apple during Steve Jobs' regime draws out at least some similarities with Huawei's 'reverse culture' tactics, inspired by the Chinese military.

- A product must remain tightly under wraps right up to its launch.
- The extra press coverage from this is worth a fortune and gives pre-release publicity free of charge, fuelled inexpensively by the rumour mill.
- The penalty for revealing Apple secrets, intentionally or unintentionally, is 'swift termination.'
- More generally, Apple reprimands its staff for talking about work, fanning the associated fear.
- Jobs is quoted to have said several times: "Anything disclosed from this meeting will result not just in termination but in prosecution to the fullest extent possible"!
- The silence and stealth mode has benefits for existing products too, as long as releases don't steal their thunder.
- Secrecy avoids giving competitors time to respond, builds customer anticipation, and avoids exposing Apple to critics ahead of time which can lead to a public bashing of an idea rather than a considered assessment of an actual product.

Jobs paid a lot of attention to secrecy in the organization and chose militaristically to use a 'scared silent' tactic with employees and managers.

Jobs was widely described as a man of Buddhism, a religion or way of life often associated with a humanistic and open culture.

Interestingly, there was much more militarism in Jobs' approach to employees as part of Apple's innovation processes than is the case in many if not all other innovative organizations. This also applied to his leadership style: it is now evident that Jobs was much closer to being a military dictator than a textbook CEO. In terms of information, this implied strict rules of confidentiality and also swift punishment if Jobs' own version of military code was not followed to the letter.

HOW PRODUCT DEVELOPMENT (e.g. OF THE iPHONE) TAKES PLACE

The innovation process at Apple is focused on product development, of course. However, there is little doubt that Steve Jobs' strategic mindset played a pivotal role in framing this product innovation and Apple's ability to execute it successfully. In recent years, the company's success hasn't just been about great products, but also about content—taking Apple into new business streams and markets it had never dealt in before. Within just a few years, the company managed to create a new ecosystem spanning music, mobility, internet, broadband, third-party applications, and more. This had become Apple's corporate strategy under Jobs' second reign.

The development of the iPhone has been a central part of this corporate strategy. In Walter Isaacson's biography of Steve Jobs, ample evidence is given of the decisive role Jobs played during the development phase. Once Jobs had decided on a handset comprising 'gorilla glass', a multi-touch screen, and many other unprecedented components, Apple eventually arrived at the design phase.

Isaacson writes:

> On many of his major projects, such as the first Toy Story and the Apple store, Jobs pressed pause as they neared completion and decided to make major revisions. That happened with the design of the iPhone as well. The initial design had the glass screen set into an aluminum case. One Monday morning Jobs went over to see Ive. "I didn't sleep last night," he said, "because I realized that I just don't love it." It was the most important product he had made since the first Macintosh, and it just didn't look right to him. Ive, to his dismay, instantly realized that Jobs was right. "I remember feeling absolutely embarrassed that he had to make the observation". . . The whole device felt too masculine, task-driven, efficient. "Guys, you've killed yourselves over

this design for the last nine months, but we're going to change it," Jobs told Ive's team. "We're all going to have to work nights and weekends."[3]

This story is illuminating in several ways—highlighting Jobs' perfectionism, control, dedication, dictatorship, and approach to execution.

THE ENFORCEMENT OF INTERNAL SECRECY

When trying to describe and explain organizational culture and behavior, it can be difficult to uncover much more than general values such as perfectionism, dictatorship, dedication etc. Yet some of Apple's organizing principles deviate so far from the standard operational behavior that it is worth trying to delve deeper into (see the adjacent box!).

The starting point for the development of the iPhone is the success of the iPod which suddenly skyrocketed in 2005, when it accounted for a whopping 45% of Apple's total revenue. On the back of this achievement, Jobs proclaimed that "The device that can eat our lunch is the cell phone . . . Everyone carries a phone, so that could render the iPod unnecessary."[4]

As a result, the initial premise was to create an iPod that could also make calls, thereby bridging the music and the cell phone industries.

As we know, the iPhone emerged as a much more advanced product, which exploded onto the market out of nowhere, thanks to a deliberate policy of internal secrecy that was as stringent and as strictly adhered to as would be

- The top 100 best staff were taken out of the base organization of many different departments.
- Rank did not confer status. An unwritten caste system applied.
- The departments did not get any information on the development project whatsoever.
- From one day to the other, staff outside the top 100 would be unable to access the same rooms as the new departments (established for developing the mobile device).
- No usual approach to delegation took place with regard to this project—Steve Jobs was instantly involved.
- Jobs' role was not to frame the work (according to usual motivation theory) but rather to give direct orders.
- Focus groups or user community testing was not utilized. Jobs defined what the users should have and what they wanted.
- Employees come to work to work. What they do at Apple is their true religion with similarities to the focus and detail of Buddhism, and the 'less is more' principle.
- Apple is fully integrated vertically, so product development is not dependent on other companies to turn the company's vision into products.
- Fewer rather than many products, avoiding feature creep and 'crabware.'
- Jobs: "The 'Innovator's Dilemma' doesn't exist at Apple."

the case in military organizations (see box)[5]. And so this black swan grew even bigger. By 2007 Jobs had brought to market three revolutionary products: an iPod with touch control, a revolutionary mobile device, and a breakthrough internet communications device. The real genius in this was that all three were encapsulated in a single, beautiful, and highly desirable device, the iPhone.

DOES THE FUTURE LOOK AS SWEET FOR APPLE?

Our intention in presenting this focus on Apple is not to provide a comprehensive description of all the company's credentials, but to highlight selected behavioral characteristics that may facilitate the understanding of Apple as a black swan.

First, it is clear that Apple pursues so-called 'reverse behavioral codices' (the company does not share information, discourages lateral thinking, encourages staff to stay within their own silo, insists on confidentiality clauses, and fosters cell-like behavior and military-like clearing procedures, etc.). The term 'reverse' is used because traditional management literature has advised at least one whole generation that the *opposite* is important—i.e. keeping staff informed and being much more inclusive and open.

- To discuss a topic at a meeting, one must be sure everyone in the room is "disclosed" on the topic meaning that they have been privy to certain secrets.
- Work organized as the cell structure where everything is strictly on a need-to-know basis only.
- Silos within silos, and security badges to ensure that employees are only allowed in certain areas, with some areas being more restrictive than others.
- Only few Apple employees have ever seen the most restrictive area, the industrial design lab where Apple's designers, the highest "caste", work.
- Employees are kept in the dark as much as possible in a cooperative environment devoid of overt politicking.
- DRI—Directly Responsible Individual.
- Top 100 was shrouded in secrecy. They were told not to put the meetings on their calendars and not to discuss it internally. Meeting rooms were swept for bugs.

Second, there is the importance attached to the element of surprise. Apple's behavioral codices are orchestrated and instituted to ensure the highest possible level of secrecy—internally as well as externally. Apple pulled off an incredible feat by keeping the iPhone under wraps throughout its conception and development—right up to the official public launch. This produced a whole series of benefits for Apple—not least maximizing exposure while minimizing the need for advertising due to word-of-mouth buzz in the market, and ensuring the highest possible levels of demand, leading to both beachhead and first-mover advantages vis-à-vis the competitors (see Table 5.1).

Table 5.1
Apple From the Paradigm Perspective

	Paradigm/ Terminology	Conventional Paradigm	Emerging Paradigm	How does the case illustrate the emerging paradigm?
The surprise dimension	Market position	Market leadership	Zero market share = perfect start	Revolutionizing in an unprecedented way through: (a) surprise tactics; (b) focus on usability; and (c) a very narrow product portfolio
The surprise dimension	Starting block	First mover, pole position, and sustainable advantages	Late or last or unexpected mover and ephemeral advantages	Surprise tactics backed up by unprecedented behavioral codex on confidentiality, clearing, and silo methods
The innovation dimension	Size of change	Marginal/ incremental	Revolutionary, unprecedented leaps	Innovation to the extreme orchestrated by a single individual (Steve Jobs)
The innovation dimension	Change mode	Differentiate and value creation	Innovate substantially, and impact tactics	The creation of new ecosystems crossing the traditional industries of music, mobility, internet, broadband, third-party applications, etc.
The X-factor dimension	Degree of rationalization	Everything explained/ planned	Focus on exploitation of the X factor (the unexplained, the unplanned, the unexpected)	Very much embodied in Steve Jobs' talents as meeting unknown demands innovatively with a reverse methodology

Given Apple's checkered history as a company, before its current market leadership in the mobile sphere, it would not be fair to simply extrapolate Apple's success indefinitely. After all, who knows what other black swans may be quietly paddling upstream, ready to make their own splash?

> Anything can change, because the smartphone revolution is still in the early stages.[6]
>
> Tim Cook

KEY REFLECTIONS

A. How much (or how little) can a single individual drive or influence the success of a company?

B. In terms of our understanding of the American culture, what are the challenges when employing behavioral codices like Apple's? What are the challenges when also comparing the 'reverse culture' of Huawei or Google?

C. Could any company orchestrate the development of a black swan business to the extent that Steve Jobs did at Apple with the iPhone invention? If not, why not?

NOTES

1 Compiled from the companies and from Merrill Lynch Global Research.
2 Ibid.
3 Isaacson, Walter (2011), *Steve Jobs*, Simon & Schuster, New York, p. 472.
4 Ibid., p. 465.
5 In addition to interviews and Isaacson's biography, the text is also partially based on Lashinsky, Adam (2012), *Inside Apple,* John Murray, London, in particular when it comes to the role of Steve Jobs and procedures behind the curtains.
6 Tim Cook, *Wall Street Journal,* June 4, 2012.

Chapter 6

Aravind—the McDonaldization of Eye Care

INTRODUCTION: HUMANITARIANISM, CAMPS, AND McDONALD'S

The Aravind Eye Care System was established in India in 1976 by the 58-year-old retired eye surgeon, Dr. Venkataswamy (Dr. V). The mission was to eliminate cataract blindness in India; at the time 15 million Indians were blind as a result of cataracts, most of them poor and located in rural areas far from hospitals. Dr. Venkataswamy's ambitions in seeking to address the situation are quite idealistic:

> Intelligence and capability are not enough. There must also be the joy of doing something beautiful. Being of service to God and humanity means going well beyond the sophistication of the best technology, to the humble demonstration of courtesy and compassion to each patient.[1]

Beginning his mission modestly with 11 beds in his own home, Dr. V and his management team have since scaled up the operation to breathtaking proportions. In a single year (between April 2010 and March 2011), the Aravind 'eye care system' helped 2,646,129 outpatients and handled 315,483 surgeries at dedicated eye hospitals. Moreover, 60% of the surgeries are free, paid for by the remaining 40%. Even the paid surgery only costs USD 18, in stark

Pro-bono patients are found through 'eye camps', of which more than 2,000 are held each year. Here, Aravind moves into rural settings to proactively seek out patients instead of waiting for them to find Aravind. At these mobile camps, Aravind doctors and nurses screen patients—a few million each year—and offer those in need of surgery the chance to have this performed for free at the nearest Aravind hospital—travel, lodging, and contrast to the USD 1,800 charged for the same procedure in North America, and the even higher costs seen in some European countries. Yet Aravind is achieving gross margins in the range of 35–50% without taking donations or charity. The astonishing profitability yielded by this highly humanitarian venture allows Aravind to invest in additional hospitals and new technology.

But how has Aravind achieved this?

The company pursues a disruptive and highly innovative scaling model, inspired by McDonald's and similar assembly-line structures, executed through a lean management system. In a way, Aravind has industrialized the surgical process and dramatically improved the productivity of its employees, equipment, and technologies.

The assembly-line system is like McDonald's, the only significant difference being that Aravind is flipping patients, not burgers. Irrespective of the stark differences in the target industry, the production system of Aravind and McDonald's share major structural similarities.

food are also included. Those accepting the offer (90% yields are typical) are transported to the hospital the same evening and operated on the following day, before being taken back to their rural villages.

Paying patients can turn up at an Aravind eye hospital without prior agreement and simply pay at the reception desk. They are given a card on which doctors will fill out information as these pre-op patients move through the screening system (six at a time). Each patient is accompanied by a nurse around a series of stations, where assessments are being carried out continuously.

Operations stretch doctors' time to the limit. Whereas the average ophthalmologist in India performs some 400 surgeries per year, an Aravind doctor will carry out around 2,000. In each Aravind facility there are four operating tables and two doctors. New patients are brought in in a constant stream; each doctor moves between his two operating tables and operates continuously.

BLACK SWAN EMERGENCE

Aravind is trust owned and a hybrid profit–non-profit organization. It is not under pressure to deliver value to owners or to grow its profit margin. Aravind continuously rechannels surplus funds into new strategic and organizational developments. Thulasiraj Ravilla, part of the leadership team at Aravind, pairs this set-up with a particular mindset:

> One needs the mindset to be wanting to give away what you have as a surplus.[2]

Aravind's McDonaldization of eye-care 'production' is truly innovative. Ravilla makes the following observation:

> I think the eyeball is the same, [in] an American or African. The problem is the same, the treatment is the same. Yet why should there be so much variation in quality and service?[3]

Today, Aravind's services span Asia, Africa, and a number of other countries through the Lions Aravind Institute of Community Ophthalmology. This tremendous success, and surprising market disruption, owes much to the company's black swan traits. Aravind had big ideas, alternative vision, and the courage to take unprecedented action to achieve a huge leap over traditional competitors. Contributing to the company's vast achievements have been the following company characteristics:

- Aravind exists for its customers, not for the company owners. The eye camps (2,000+ a year) move out into rural settings to *find* patients. Patients in need are then transported free of charge to and from the hospital. *Increasing rather than reducing the number of potential customers!*
- Aravind models its social and health-care service on the product assembly-line operations of McDonald's or a best-in-class manufacturer. *Reducing production costs by increased productivity!*
- Nurses are undereducated local young women selected for a free two-year education at Aravind. They are guaranteed work at Aravind afterwards. This gives Aravind the educated staff it needs, at a local salary. The competitive salary keeps Aravind's costs down and makes it possible to have sufficient staff for the assembly-line structure to work smoothly. *Combining high motivation and low labor costs!*
- In response to high product prices of the required eye lenses, Aravind has funded its own solutions, investing in Aurolab and the invention of an USD 8 lens (in contrast to the USD 150 lenses on the US market). Crucially, it insisted on matching the high quality of incumbent products. Aurolab is trust owned and its IOC lenses command 10% market share globally. Aurolab products have multiplied and are exported to 130 countries, with target markets including India, Africa, Latin America, Central America, and Southeast Asia. Aurolab also envisages entering European and other developed markets. *Breaking the monopolistic delivery structures to achieve dramatically reduced costs!*
- Constantly driven by the goal to reach and help more people, Aravind is keenly focused on scale. There is an ongoing drive to screen and operate to an ever greater degree, and to make products for less, so that the mission to eliminate blindness can be fulfilled. *Employing 'man-on-the-moon' innovative thinking to accomplish a difficult mission!*
- Applying learning-by-doing experiments in line with a tangible vision. The latest example can be seen in Aravind's attempt to multiply surgeries from

270,000 a year in 2006 to 0.5 million a year in 2015. The strategy for this is a 'managed hospital' approach, whereby Aravind partners with proprietary staff to manage eye hospitals other than its own. This is currently being piloted in three hospitals. *Franchising-like ideas in order to proliferate!*

Aravind's model may eventually challenge the way all hospitals and surgeries operate in industrially developed countries. In this way the company provides an empirical example of the emergence of a new paradigm, as depicted in Table 6.1.

Table 6.1
Aravind From the Paradigm Perspective

	Paradigm/ Terminology	Conventional Paradigm	Emerging Paradigm	How does the case illustrate the emerging paradigm?
The surprise dimension	Market position	Market leadership	Zero market share = perfect start	From 11 beds in Dr. V's own home, to 300,000 annual surgeries
The innovation dimension	Change mode	Differentiate and value creation	Innovate substantially and impact tactics	Changing the structures and markets of eye surgery. Assembly-line system (McDonaldization) mixed with a social mission and healthcare services[4]
The innovation dimension	Methodology	Analytical	Passionate	Idealistic and mission-driven man-on-the moon innovation
The cost dimension	Cost structure	Conventional cost structure	Disruptive cost structure	Production costs are marginal compared with Western eye surgery. Trust owned = rechanneling surplus into new innovations which lower costs further

(Continued)

**Table 6.1
(Continued)**

	Paradigm/ Terminology	Conventional Paradigm	Emerging Paradigm	How does the case illustrate the emerging paradigm?
The X-factor dimension	Degree of rationalization	Everything explained/ planned	Focus on exploitation of the X factor (the unexplained, the unplanned, the unexpected)	Eye camps, on-the-spot surgery, cheaper innovative lenses
The regulatory dimension	Governmental support	Marginally or not addressed	National subsidies, home market, or cultural advantages	Works with NGOs, researchers, and governmental offices to enhance efficiency and achieve quality of service/products

KEY REFLECTIONS

A. Does big-leap innovation have more potential for success in an emerging economy versus an industrially developed economy?

B. How could some of the reverse thinking illustrated in the Aravind case be applied in the health sector outside of India, and in other markets besides the health industry?

C. Try to expand on 2–3 scenarios, describing the likely effect on the health sector in for example the US or Europe if Aravind were to set up operations in these countries, or if its model were transferred to and executed by other health organizations in those regions.

NOTES

1 Dr. Govindappa Venkataswamy, Aravind Eyecare Systems' homepage, www.aravind.org/aboutus, September 2013.
2 Thulasiraj Ravilla (Executive Director of LAICO, Aravind Eye Care System); excerpt from TED India, November 1, 2009.
3 Ibid.
4 More detail on the assembly-line functions employed by Aravind is provided in Díaz, Pons, and Pahls (2010), IE Business School case study.

Chapter 7

Emirates Airlines— Globalization from the Desert

Emirates is one of the fastest growing and most profitable airlines in the world. Yet the secret of its success is largely unknown outside the Arab world. It is necessary to look at the inner workings of the company to comprehend how strategically important its HQ location in Dubai is, and the extent to which the choice of a desert as the central hub of its operations deviates from conventional strategy thinking.

HOW IT ALL BEGAN

As has been the case for the few successful non-state airlines, Emirates was born out of a crisis. In 1985 Gulf Air refused to increase flights to and from Dubai unless the government protected the carrier's long-haul services. This was all the motivation Sheikh Mohammed bin Rashid Al-Maktoum needed. Instead of trying to persuade Gulf Air to change its mind, he established the Emirates Airlines knowing how dependent Dubai was on air travel.

To lead the venture he hired Emirates' first CEO, Maurice Flanagan from the UK, who, after a long career with British Airways, had taken up a role at Dubai travel and airport organization Dnata.

Right from the start, Emirates did things differently. The Sheikh instructed Flanagan:

> Forget about protection against competition. That's not the way Dubai works.[1]

Flanagan built a team together with the appointed chairman, Sheikh Ahmed bin Saeed Al Maktoum. One strategic appointment was Tim Clark, from Gulf Air, as head of airline planning. Clark had built up a reputation as a very strong route planner. The company set up with a loan of USD 10 million (since paid back many times over) and two leased planes, to fly a Dubai–Karachi route that had not existed previously. Within a year, Emirates was flying to Bombay and Delhi and quickly expanded to encompass destinations such as Colombo, Dhaka, Amman, and Cairo

(1986), Frankfurt and Istanbul (1987), and Asian locations including Bangkok, Manila, and Singapore (1989).

The company quickly disrupted business for its nearest competitor, Gulf Air, which in the first year of Emirates' existence suffered a 30% loss.

Emirates did not receive any direct subsidies, nor did it rely on government handouts, according to prevailing reports. Dubai's 'open skies' policy granted foreign airlines the same access and privileges as Emirates. Operating under this policy has been a cornerstone in the competitive game, according to Flanagan, who has commented that:

> This has helped us to become a carrier which can compete with the best of the world's airlines.[2]

Emirates has thrived since its foundation, enjoying an annual growth rate in the order of 25%, making it the world's largest carrier. The business is divided into a number of companies—first and foremost the Emirates airline itself, with subsidiaries in resorts, congresses, and holiday tours, as well as divisions such as Emirates SkyCargo (with its own soaring success), Emirates Aviation College, and Emirates Engineering.

By 2011, Emirates was the largest airline company in the world in terms of scheduled international passenger kilometers flown. By 2012 it was operating on six continents and flying to 111 destinations, carrying more than 31 million passengers a year. In May 2012, Emirates announced its

The Fuel Issue

Being owned by the government of Dubai, Emirates has been accused of getting fuel at reduced prices, sponsored directly by the Dubai sheikhs. President Tim Clark has refuted this allegation numerous times. In his speech to the European Aviation Club in 2009, he lashed out:

> The other claim we hear ad nauseam, usually fired from a grassy knoll in the Frankfurt area, is our secret supply of free fuel. I imagine this comes from the somewhat simplistic view that all Gulf States are oil rich and therefore must have fuel pumps dispensing giveaway Avgas. The truth is that we, like almost all other airlines, buy fuel on the open market from multiple global suppliers. The jet fuel price paid by Emirates at Dubai Airport is based on the Arab Gulf jet fuel traded in Singapore . . . And the price we pay in Paris, Frankfurt or Heathrow is courtesy of these well-known European charities, Royal Dutch Shell and British Petroleum.

In the financial year 2007/2008, fuel accounted for more than 30% of Emirates' total expenditure, comparable with other international long-haul carriers such as British Airways, Lufthansa, Qantas, or Singapore Airlines (http://en.wikipedia.org/wiki/Emirates_business_model).

At the time of writing, Emirates' fuel costs had in the most recent accounts added up to 34.4% of its total operating costs, rising to 45% for the current period, with prospects of further increases to come (www.bloomberg.com/news/2012-03-21/emirates-says-whole-load-of-airlines-will-fail-in-fuel-squeeze.html).

To address the fuel price challenge, which is one of the key factors contributing to the steady flow of bankruptcies being witnessed

24th consecutive year of profit, up by almost 18% from the previous year—highly impressive in a sector in crisis.

The core story behind Emirates' success is the visionary route planning and its understanding of changing markets and geographies. From initially being considered a geographical outlier in the desert, Emirates has reversed this perspective to position Dubai as a deliberate global hub. The competitors regularly accuse Emirates of being protected by the Dubai government ownership through competition-distorting subsidies and free or very cheap oil supplies. However, Emirates consistently presents accounts which refute these claims.

> in the airline industry, Emirates has invested in the latest and lightest energy-conserving aircraft. Its fuel efficiency rates are currently 30% below the global fleet average, and continued improvements are being made on the numerous new planes on order with Boeing and Airbus.

REINVENTING DUBAI

Much of Emirates' success is due to Sheikh Ahmed bin Saeed Al Maktoum's ambitious strategy of reinventing Dubai as a modern hub of business and tourism in the Middle East. This is reflected in one of the company's slogans:

> Fly Emirates, meet Dubai.

Tim Clark, now president of the airline, attributes Emirates' achievements to a deep understanding of how the world is connected—not only today but also in the future, and the benefit of locating its central hub at its home airport in Dubai.

The support of ambitious home-rulers cannot be underestimated either: they have built Dubai from a dusty desert post in the 1970s to one of the world's most bustling centers of growth, finance, and business connections. In 2010, the number of visitors was approximately 15 million with another 20 million travelers passing through Dubai in transit. This further fuels the expansion of Emirates which will contribute to and benefit from the growth.

REJECTING CONVENTIONAL WISDOM

Emirates' recipe for success cannot be found in any conventional management book. The company's creative approach to seizing opportunities and solving problems can be attributed to a distinct mindset, according to former CEO Maurice Flanagan, who famously noted:

> We don't have to do what other airlines do.[3]

Another contributing characteristic is Emirates' flexible organization which favors an informal and entrepreneurial spirit. The company's family-based structure provides the airline with great structural flexibility.

Gary Chapman, president of the affiliated company Dnata, has summarized Emirates' success as follows:

> Emirates [is] organized around the strengths of individuals rather than [the constraints of] rigid organizational structure.[4]

Emirates' strategy and decision-making process seems to follow a fluid approach—one more akin to that of a start-up than to a traditional airline carrier with rigid layers and procedures. A simple 'Okay' from the Sheikh suffices. This is the Dubai style, Flanagan argues:

> Obviously, you must have created the confidence to get into that situation. We have weekly meetings, and the ability to go to the Sheikh or to the senior management group and get a decision very quickly is the key.[5]

Emirates has become something of an *enfant terrible* in the airline industry. It consistently argues against restrictions on market access, airport usage, and airline ownership, not least in the form of alliances and national/regional protection laws. Star Alliance, OneWorld, and SkyTeam are the world's three largest alliances, covering 47–66% of North American and European markets. Emirates briefly considered joining StarAlliance in 2000, but decided (strongly) against it on the grounds that its strategic freedom would be hindered.

Since then, Emirates has risen as a harsh critic of protectionism by alliances and nations. Dubai airport, Emirates' home base, remains an 'open skies' territory—meaning that no airlines are prevented from using it. But other airports are hard to negotiate access to—it took Emirates three years to gain a foothold in Australian airports such as Sydney, for example. Also, EU regulations and German protectionism have led to tough battles for Emirates. Driven by the interests of the alliances to which their largest home operators belong, national authorities have put pressure on Emirates—take, for example, Germany where the company was forced to increase its prices so as to not be too competitive for Lufthansa! Emirates pursues its anti-regulation mission with lawsuits, very transparent reporting, and provocative discussions and statements to the aviation community.

THE GOVERNMENT–SHEIKH SUBSIDIES ISSUE

Emirates' business model has been repeatedly queried, with allegations that the airline's aggressive fleet investments over the years—even in times of adversity—cannot possibly have been supported by its earnings alone. In 2005, the CEO of Air France–KLM Group, Leo van Wijk, spoke in blunt terms at an annual industry gathering, saying: "Many of us have great doubts about how Emirates is paying for these A380s when your cash flow isn't big enough to support it. So where do you get the money?"[6]

Implied was significant sponsorship by the Dubai government, which would be against market competition laws. The now president, Tim Clark, has subsequently responded by noting first that other airlines are government owned, too—e.g. Air New Zealand, Finnair, and Singapore Airlines. Second, Emirates pays the same price as other airlines at its hub in Dubai.

It is the fact that Dubai is also Emirates' own base that provides an important indicator to the source of the company's success. While passenger traffic worldwide decreases, it increases in Dubai and the growth of the country as an international hub has boosted the success of the airline immensely. Furthermore, Emirates has a route network which caters to millions of people who would otherwise have to fly via third destinations. The sheer genius of the Dubai location means that Emirates can reach 75% of all destinations within an eight-hour flight. It is, in Clark's words, "an ultra-competitive aviation honey pot."[7]

Canadian Accusations

Emirates' financial auditor, PricewaterhouseCoopers (PwC), has revealed nothing in the company accounts that suggests government subsidies or similar. Meanwhile a report from UBS Investment concurs that it "can find little evidence of any subsidies."

But these assurances have done little to slow down the rumour mill. In 2011, Emirates was forced to respond to accusations from Canada's prime minister, no less. Tim Clark did this by way of an open letter. This stated:

> I challenge Prime Minister Harper or any member of his government to produce one shred of evidence to support the false accusations which are repeatedly reported as fact by the Canadian media. We have stated on many occasions that Emirates is not subsidised in any way, shape or form by the Dubai government: it never has been and never will be. Our financial statements audited by PricewaterhouseCoopers, the world's largest accounting firm, confirm that there is no evidence of subsidisation whatsoever. These accounts have been made freely available to the public through Emirates' website (www.emirates.com) and they clearly demonstrate that we do not receive any direct or indirect subsidies.

(www.newswire.ca/en/story/743881/letter-from-tim-clark-president-of-emirates-airline)

In response to the steadily incoming accusations of fraud, Emirates has adopted a staunch open-market position, pointing out the hidden 'subsidies' and/or protectionism embedded in many alliances and national models. This is part of Emirates' brand today—OPEN. Group chairman and CEO Ahmed bin Saeed Al Maktoum states in the airline's 2010/11 annual report: "OPEN is . . . the foundation of our core, long-term business strategy. Quite frankly, placing restrictions on airline ownership and market access is incongruent to how the rest of the business world works in the 21st century."[8] OPEN goes hand in hand with the open-skies policy.

DEVELOPMENT FROM THE DESERT

As many reports in the business consultancy press discuss (e.g. EIU's *Global Disruptors,* 2008; BCG's *Companies on the Move,* 2011; BCG's *Unlocking Growth in the Middle,* 2012; and IBM's *Global CEO* study), emerging markets are the place to be for tomorrow's (and today's) corporation. Asia & the Gulf have been called 'the new Silk Road' (McKinsey Quarterly, 2006), the argument being that those able to create the products, services, and travels for that road will win the future. Emirates do this by catering not to the old West, but to holidaymakers and business personnel from localities neglected by incumbents.

Emirates understood this new connectivity pattern from an early stage. As Clark put it in his speech to the European Aviation Club in 2009:

> Aviation *is* the globalised world and air services helped to make the earth flat. Our model works because we don't have a one-dimensional route network of traditional Atlantic or Pacific crossings, or just the Kangaroo route or focusing inside one region. Connecting *Moscow to Durban,* or *Beijing to Luanda,* or *Hyderabad to LA,* or *Perth to Dubai,* are some of the thousands of examples of the new world's city pairs.

Residing within 4,000 miles of Dubai—roughly an eight-hour flight on today's modern jetliners—are 3.5 billion people (more than half of the world's population) and 75% of all destinations. Before any other airline discovered the opportunity, Emirates capitalized on its location and created a hub to connect all of these people.

Emirates took advantage of starting out as a nobody. Neither Emirates nor Dubai were considered important regional players, and it was easy for Emirates to negotiate airport access both in and beyond its regional domain. During its first three years, the three top executives (Clark, Ahmed, and Flanagan) travelled to numerous destinations to negotiate traffic rights with governments, speak with key opinion leaders and construct the future route network. As described by a CNN journalist:

> Believing that the airline would never amount to much, most foreign governments were happy to give it access to their runways.[9]

Right from the start, the top Emirates team combined a full understanding of the incumbent carriers and the dual opportunity presented by the desert location of the company (i.e. that Emirates' master plan could be developed and fulfilled away from international attention, and that this location would emerge as the unexpected center of a new global web of flight routes). Together these strengths gave Emirates a solid background from which to launch a strong, unnoticed, black swan disruption strategy.

Moreover, Emirates has grown in line with Dubai itself. The vision of the Sheikh to build Dubai into a world business hub was closely tied to the need for an airline and airport that could support this connectivity. In this way, the airline has been part of a larger institutional structure from its very beginning, to the mutual benefit of Emirates and the Emirate of Dubai.

The Sheikh also molded Dubai's aviation policy to be supportive of a flight carrier choosing Dubai as its home airport. Specifically, this dictated that:

> Dubai's airport would be open around the clock. Unlike most destination cities, which abide by noise restrictions, Dubai hosts landings and takeoffs at any hour. That means that Emirates can keep its fleet in the air an average of nearly 14 hours a day, compared with 11 for many rivals. At an average cost of USD 150,000 per hour to maintain a plane on the ground that translates into tens of millions of dollars in annual savings.[10]

Partly because of the Dubai location, partly because of efficiency and productivity, Emirates' labor costs tie up just 18% of the airline's operating budget, compared with 27% for Lufthansa and 29% for United Airlines—not least due to its access to cheap labor from India and Pakistan.

According to much conventional thinking, successful intercontinental airlines emanate primarily from the US, secondarily from the larger countries of Europe. Based in the Middle Eastern desert, Emirates has turned this assumption upside down, supporting the emerging paradigm with the unexpected element of geographical location as a decisive X factor (see Table 7.1).

Table 7.1
Emirates From the Paradigm Perspective

	Paradigm/ Terminology	Conventional Paradigm	Emerging Paradigm	How does the case illustrate the emerging paradigm?
The surprise dimension	Market position	Market leadership	Zero market share = perfect start	Zero market share. Fringe, clean slate, starter from the desert *(Continued)*

Table 7.1 (Continued)

	Paradigm/ Terminology	Conventional Paradigm	Emerging Paradigm	How does the case illustrate the emerging paradigm?
The surprise dimension	Starting block	First mover, pole position, and sustainable advantages	Late or last or unexpected mover and ephemeral advantages	Unexpected— because of disruptive route network not having been spotted by incumbents
The innovation dimension	Change mode	Differentiate and value creation	Innovate substantially and impact tactics	Changes global travelling trajectories with new route network. Turns route thinking upside down
The innovation dimension	Benchmarking technology	Best practice	Next practice	Youngest fleet in the world— invests in new technology and fuel reductions
The X-factor dimension	Degree of rationalization	Everything explained/ planned	Focus on exploitation of the X factor (the unexplained, the unplanned, the unexpected)	Dubai desert location as the exploitable X factor
The regulatory dimension	Governmental support	Marginally or not addressed	National subsidies, home market, or cultural advantages	100% government owned. State growth = airline growth. Takes advantage of being part of the ambitious national strategy and the push for open skies

KEY REFLECTIONS

A. A driving force in the development of the Emirates has been the goal not only to develop a global airline but also to create a new focus on Dubai as the hub of the world. In this way Emirates and Dubai's governors have aligned ambitions and mutual benefits. Is this typical for a city and an airline? Can you think of other potential win-wins between companies and their geographical locations?

B. Emirates, like Ryanair, has demonstrated that going against the wind and subscribing to non-conventional wisdom pays off. This can be characterized as an X-factor mindset and a stand-out ability to reverse the conventional modus operandi.

C. From a management perspective, the case of Emirates also indicates a kind of reverse globalization, showing how an airline originating in a desert in the Middle East can, from nothing, almost conquer the world. Is there a danger that Western companies are underestimating peers from emerging economies? Will we see more Emirates in the future?

NOTES

1 Quoted from Sull, Donald N., Ghoshal, Sumantra, and Monteiro, Felipe (2005), The hub of the world, *Business Strategy Review,* Spring.
2 Ibid.
3 Ibid.
4 Ibid.
5 Ibid.
6 See Maier, Matthew (2005), Rise of the Emirates' empire, *CNN Money,* October 1.
7 Clark, Tim (2005), speech to the European Aviation Club, 12 November.
8 See Emirates Annual Report (2010/2011).
9 See Maier, Matthew (2005), Rise of the Emirates empire, *CNN Money,* October 1.
10 Ibid.

Chapter 8

Huawei—Countryside Surrounding Cities

Chinese companies have started to win first place in global markets. Huawei has just overtaken Sweden's Ericsson to become the world's largest telecoms equipment maker. Even though many foreigners still cannot pronounce its name (some call it "Hawaii," and the firm has even produced a video teaching people to say hwah-way), Huawei is becoming an increasingly powerful global player, capable of going head-to-head with the best in intensely competitive markets. It follows Haier, which is already the leading white goods maker; now Lenovo is challenging Hewlett-Packard as the world's biggest PC-maker. Plenty more will follow.[1]

OUTLIER AND BLACK SWAN

Earlier in the book we spoke a lot about the power of being an outlier; it is, after all, how black swans are able to creep up on the unsuspecting inhabitants of an established environment. They wait out of sight and, when they are ready, make a great splash. Chinese telecoms equipment manufacturer Huawei is a great example of an outlier in several respects.

In general terms, the case of Huawei is one of swift transformation. In 1987 the company was certainly an outlier, being an unknown start-up in China; by 2012 it was global market leader in its chosen field. But how did it get from A to B? Capitalizing on its position as an outlier was clearly a part of this strategy. But there is more to Huawei's story than that.

Looking at the inner workings of Huawei reveals some rather unprecedented strategic components. One is borrowed from the Chinese military—the idea that an effective approach when trying to capture a city is to first capture the countryside around it.

Huawei has applied this 'countryside surrounding cities' strategy to its target markets and customer bases. While the mantra of many global companies today is to first go after the most lucrative markets and richest customers, Huawei has reversed this by initially pursuing some of the apparently least attractive customer bases. This reverse strategy has caught some incumbent technology suppliers by surprise, and has successfully paved the way for deals with richer markets and more prestigious customers as success and interest has spread.

This isn't the only example of out-of-the-box thinking exhibited by Huawei. The company has also challenged standard management principles in the way it operates internally; specifically it favors comprehensive employee stock ownership and a collectivistic 'wolf' culture which is described later in this chapter.

In this sense, Huawei is not simply an outlier. It is fully-fledged black swan, which has perfectly honed the element of surprise by being prepared to do things differently. Let's now examine these respective traits in more detail.

A BLACK SWAN EMERGES

As recently as a decade ago Huawei was not even on the telecom equipment industry radar, in a business populated by companies typically with a track record of 100 years or more; in just a few years it has come from almost nowhere to dominate its chosen market (see Figure 8.1).

For many years, Huawei was regarded as little more than a local Chinese vendor; in 2004 the company wasn't even among the top 10 globally. But just three years later, it suddenly emerged as number four by revenue, growing to become number three in 2008 and number two in 2010. By 2012 Huawei was number one by corporate revenue, and its growth was no longer confined to the Chinese market.

Today, approximately 140,000 employees work in this privately owned company, of which as many as 46% are reported to work in research and development.

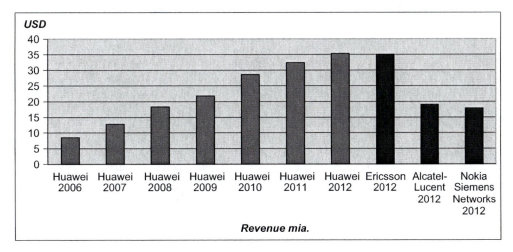

FIGURE 8.1 Huawei's Growth (2006–2012)[2]

To go from almost zero to number one in this hugely complex oligopolistic environment in less than a decade is a phenomenally rapid development when compared with the fact that it took 20 years to develop and implement the GSM standard, 10 years to develop and commercialize 3G and another 10 years to develop and commercialize the 4G standard. Huawei was not even delivering GSM equipment when the mobile opportunity emerged in the early nineties. This being the case, it would be an understatement to characterize Huawei as merely an outlier; rather, the company is a pure black swan.

A closer look at some of the key components of this breathtaking development provides some explanation.

MILITARY PRECISION

Huawei's strategy of metaphorically taking its target cities by first capturing the surrounding countryside has been a key component of the company's success. Its goal initially was to achieve sufficient domination of developing countries so that it could later challenge and overcome the fortress of vendors delivering to blue-chip customers in more developed countries.

The 'countryside surrounding cities' principle was originally devised by Mao Zedong, the first president of the People's Republic of China. Mao's thinking was that if you can beat the enemy in the countryside where they are weak, you will become stronger and eventually be able to win in the city. In the case of Huawei's geographic strategy, the African market and developing countries in general represent the countryside and the richest Western countries, where GSM originated, the cities.

Huawei's success may have been quick and highly disruptive, but it has not been wholly straightforward. For several years Huawei has effectively been frozen out of the US market due to US government concerns about security (such as illegal tapping of telephone calls).

Relations between China and the West are strained at the best of times when it comes to matters of information management and communication, and the possibility of unwanted state intervention. It isn't

- Adopting a 'countryside surrounding cities' strategy, i.e. focusing initially on developing countries (e.g. Africa) where the 'enemy' is weak, i.e. building up a 'black swan' effect.
- Establishing numerous partnerships with recognized Western companies, such as IBM, Symantec, Siemens, and others.
- Claiming to expend 62,000 employees (the Ericsson rival quotes to expend 22,000 by comparison) on R&D and possessing a very strong base of patents.
- Disruptive cost structure, due to e.g. cheap labor, flows through to low prices for the clients.
- Present in many of the same countries where the Chinese

just the US that is nervous about using a Chinese company to supply communications infrastructure. In March 2012 the Australian government excluded Huawei from tendering for contracts connected with its National Broadband Network following advice based on security concerns.

But it is the US embargo that has most perturbed Huawei, especially following a US Congress committee report which was interpreted as attacking China. This elicited the following response from the Chinese government:

government establishes cooperative programs.
- A USD 30 billion credit line from China Development Bank for the benefit of Huawei's clients.
- 'Surrounding countryside' well achieved as number one in developing countries— 'surrounding cities' materializing with a number of attractive contracts in Europe.

> This report by the relevant committee of the US Congress, based on subjective suspicions, has no solid foundation and, on the grounds of national security, has made groundless accusations against China.[3]

The worst-case scenario is an out-and-out trade war:

> Can you imagine if China started asking US companies coming to China what their relationship was with the Democratic or Republican parties? It would be a mess. If you see me as a Trojan horse, how should I view you?[4]

Huawei is also accused of anti-competitive behavior, predatory pricing, and subsidies, in particular with regard to EU regulation. The EU Commission launched an inquiry in 2010–2011 into whether China was giving illegal aid to Huawei and ZTE, following a complaint. When the complaint was withdrawn, the Commission said it would be "disproportionate to continue with the investigation,"[5] but in May 2012 the media reported that the EU was going to open a trade case against Huawei and ZTE, alleging that they had obtained illegal governmental subsidies and sold products in the EU below costs. Somewhat surprisingly, rival Ericsson indicated that it opposes a planned probe by the EU Commission, stating that "an anti-dumping case . . . that could potentially lead to punitive import tariffs being imposed on them . . . was the wrong way to proceed."[6]

It is worth noting that Ericsson, in recent years, has won substantial similar business in China.

Both the US "embargo" and the (potential) Huawei–EU case displays in a sense how successful the 'countryside surrounding cities' strategy has evolved. By now, Huawei has become hugely successful in the "countryside" and is increasingly becoming successful in the "cities", meeting with some conflicts and resistance in the US, Australia, and partly the EU.

HUAWEI FROM THE INSIDE – THE CREATION OF A REVERSE CULTURE

Huawei was founded by Ren Zhengfei whose background is with the Chinese military. To some extent this may have influenced the culture of Huawei. Zhengfei frequently cites Mao Zedong's thoughts in his speeches and internal publications; an internal employee magazine is called *Huawei People;* and the sales teams are referred to as 'market guerrillas.' In addition, Zhengfei urges staff to draw inspiration from the Japanese and the German work culture, as indicated in a letter from 1994 to new hires:

> I hope you abandon the mentality of achieving quick results, learn from the Japanese down-to-earth attitude and the German's spirit of being scrupulous [about] every detail.[7]

Over the years, Zhengei and Huawei have crafted a reverse culture compared with that seen in many Western companies, including some of Huawei's peers. Where many Western companies are characterized by an individualistic culture based on predominantly external shareholder ownership, bureaucratic leadership structures and styles, Huawei has found its own way, going against the grain.

Huawei is privately owned, almost exclusively by its employees, with an undisclosed share of the company still owned by Zhengfei himself. Employee ownership spans the organization, including middle managers.

Individualism is eliminated by the promotion of collectivism through the idea of hunting in packs, as wolves do. Huawei employees are taught that wolves have a keen sense of smell, are aggressive, and advance towards their prey in packs. This is also in keeping with the militaristic principle of market guerrillas. The underlying philosophy beneath employee ownership and this pack-like behavior is that everyone is in it together, and the interests of the collective outweigh those of the individual.

HUAWEI FROM THE OUTSIDE IN

At a corporate level the policy of surrounding cities by first taking the countryside, and the collectivist culture, appear to have worked well for Huawei, with implications for other would-be black swans—certainly in China.

The company's position has been further galvanized by a few other characteristics which we haven't really touched on here. These include having one of the world's largest portfolios of patents, and Huawei's approach to technology and innovation in general. For example, Huawei was the first vendor to opt 'all in' for IP standards. Invariably, this has proved to be a winning technology strategy and a helping hand to the entire company, which benefits from being unconstrained by 'old' technology.

Huawei makes for an interesting black swan, with plenty to support the emergence of a new paradigm for corporate strategy (see Table 8.1).

Table 8.1
Huawei From the Paradigm Perspective

	Paradigm/ Terminology	Conventional Paradigm	Emerging Paradigm	How does the case illustrate the emerging paradigm?
The surprise dimension	Market position	Market leadership	Zero market share = perfect start	From a position as largely unknown 5–8 years ago to becoming number one in one of the largest global industries
The surprise dimension	Starting block	First mover, pole position, and sustainable advantages	Late or last or unexpected mover and ephemeral advantages	In practice a 'last mover', piggy-backing on the comparative advantage of having an initial proprietary home market of considerable size
The innovation dimension	Change mode	Differentiate and value creation	Innovate substantially and impact tactics	One of the world's largest portfolio of patents
The innovation dimension	Size of change	Marginal/ incremental	Revolutionary, unprecedented leaps	Huawei based on IP technology from the outset
The innovation dimension	Methodology	Analytical	Passionate	Wolf culture

(Continued)

Table 8.1
(Continued)

	Paradigm/ Terminology	Conventional Paradigm	Emerging Paradigm	How does the case illustrate the emerging paradigm?
The cost dimension	Cost structure	Conventional cost structure	Disruptive cost structure	Unbeatable cost structure based on 'Chinese' prices and on top of that attractive state financed credit facilities for the customers
The X-factor dimension	Degree of rationalization	Everything explained/ planned	Focus on exploitation of the X factor (the unexplained, the unplanned, the unexpected)	Reverse culture, reverse strategy (countryside surrounding cities) leading to unprecedented cost structure, unprecedented pricing/financing vis-à-vis customers
The regulatory dimension	Market perfection	Market forces	Regulatory distortions/ wins	Huawei often wins in combination with interstate agreements covering Chinese infrastructure deliveries (like Huawei's) in exchange for oil. Furthermore, state-financed credit facilities for customers
The regulatory dimension	Regulatory forbearance	Marginally or not addressed	Regulatory game changing	Interstate agreements
The regulatory dimension	Governmental support	Marginally or not addressed	National subsidies, home market, or cultural advantages	A helping hand from the Chinese government (interstate agreements, credit facilities and, initially, a large home market)

KEY REFLECTIONS

A. A greater understanding of Chinese state funding or credit facilities could be relevant. Also, given that such could make Huawei vulnerable to national/ governmental preferences, what is the company's strategy for balancing autonomy and state support?

B. The 'pack of wolves' mindset seems pivotal for the company. Could this function well in other companies on a standalone basis or is it necessary to combine the wolf culture with employee ownership and 'countryside surrounding cities' like strategies?

C. What is the limit to Huawei's success—for how many years can the company continue to grow at a rate of 30–40% a year?

NOTES

1 *The Economist*, 4 August, 2012.
2 Own compilation of data from annual reports and public accounts.
3 Shen Danyang, a spokesman for China's Commerce Ministry 2012 (see Reuters.com, China rejects US accusations against telecoms firms, 9 October, 2012).
4 Commerce Minister Chen Deming 2012 (see Reuters.com, China derides US "Cold War mentality towards telecoms firm Huawei," November 10, 2012).
5 Reuters.co.uk, EU to end Chinese telecom probe despite subsidies, February 4, 2011.
6 Telecomlead.com, Huawei denies benefit from illegal Chinese subsidies, May 29, 2012.
7 Andersen, Froholt, and Poulfelt (2010), *Return on Strategy*, p. 164.

Chapter 9

Natura—Globalizing Beauty!

WHY NATURA GOT STARTED?

Brazil's Natura Cosméticos[1] was founded in 1969 as a protest against the traditional, highly chemical cosmetics industry. The founder, Luiz Antonio Seabra, started a small laboratory and shop in his Sao Paolo garage. The idea was to produce cosmetics that would support inner as well as outer beauty, and personal well-being as well as healthy relationships with others. Natura is a highly ideological company, presenting its corporate beliefs with the following words:

> Life is a chain of relationships. Nothing in the universe exists alone. Everything is interdependent. It is our belief that the appreciation of the importance of relationships is the foundation of an enormous human revolution in the search for peace, solidarity and life in all its manifestations.[2]

Natura has built an image as an eco-friendly, sustainable company (using natural products, working towards sustainable environment, and social support, etc.). The company also prides itself on strong research and development activity. It uses ordinary women rather than supermodels in its advertisements.

In the early 1990s, Natura stated that its raison d'être was to create and sell products that would promote 'well-being' and 'being well.' It defined the former as the harmonious and pleasant relationship we have with ourselves, the latter as the empathetic, successful and gratifying relationship we enjoy with nature and the wider environment. In 1992 Natura launched its "Truly Beautiful Woman" campaign based on the idea that feminine beauty does not depend on being young forever; rather, true beauty emanates from self-esteem and from living a healthy and meaningful life.

This highly ideological approach coexists with an intensive pursuit of growth, which has made the company a market leader in Brazil, and its stock an attractive investment. The links between these two apparent mindsets—social improvement and economic competitiveness—can be found in Natura's two core organizational features: its direct sales model and its stakeholder approach.

BRAND VALUE

Natura's business model is based on direct sales, and has been so since 1974. In this model, sales of products are made from person to person allowing the company to foster relationships and rapidly increase distribution at an extremely low cost. The word-of-mouth and user testimonials have reinforced the brand and have become Natura's main marketing tool. In 2012, the company had more than 1.2 million 'consultants' (resellers) spread throughout Argentina, Brazil, Chile, Colombia, France, Mexico, Peru, the US, Australia, and the UK among other countries, and since 2006 its sales have surpassed those of Avon in Brazil. The sales consultants handle a portfolio of over 700 products, and with an annual turnover of the sales consultants is USD 300,000, they are still seen as loyal and extremely valuable to the company. From 2007 to 2011, the number of sales consultants doubled, "boosting product orders from a telling $9 million to $17 million a year,"[3] according to Natura's manager for partnerships and tech innovation, Luciana Hashiba. In economic terms, this meant a rise in pretax earnings from USD 380 to USD 760 million and a net revenue rise from USD 1.6 to USD 2.7 billion.

Natura is exceptional. By any measure it is a giant in the industry: its 2010 net revenues of USD 2.8 billion position it among the world's top 20 beauty companies. Its USD 660 million in pretax profits, which represents a stunning margin of 24.5%, put it among the most profitable (well above Avon's 12%, Estée Lauder's 18%, and L'Oréal's 19%).

Over the last five years, the Natura brand has been highlighted as one of the most valuable, admired, and desired by Brazil's research institutes and media outlets. According to *Istoé Dinheiro* magazine, Natura was one of the most valuable brands in Brazil in 2008, not just in the business of ethics and aesthetics, as the company defines its market.

Many of Natura's sales consultants come from less privileged backgrounds, but are provided with ample training. When the company implemented a direct sales model back in 1974, a large part of the motivation was to provide decent job opportunities for women. It is a deliberate move on Natura's part that women and underprivileged people work for the company (as independent consultants) as well as being part of the social mission of Natura. Their average monthly salary is 16 times the national minimum.

Natura's direct sales have also become a factor for social change, and for financially empowering middle-class housewives, independent professionals, and low-ranked corporate staff. No experience, formal contract, or starting capital is required to become an independent Natura salesperson. This flexibility has made the sales model an attractive alternative for many households looking to supplement their existing income.

By employing sales consultants from working-class backgrounds, who have some form of disability, or who live in the slums, Natura is able to reach groups of customers it would find inaccessible otherwise. The market it has created cannot be easily replicated or penetrated by competitors. It relies on community proximity and takes effort to build. For example, through its Communities Project, Natura was able (in 2011) to reach new consultants in two of the poorest neighborhoods in Rio de Janeiro. Field research showed that many of those interested in working for Natura were prevented from applying because of financial or personal issues. By allowing applicants to have debts when they applied, and by supporting these new consultants with micro-credit and financial education, Natura boosted enrolment by 75% in these areas. Through partnerships with banks, NGOs, and relevant authorities, Natura is able not just to open up and profit from these hard-to-access markets, but also to improve them. The company grants both seed and growth funding to local sales consultants who wish to create a social project in their area. These projects have social and environmental impact, while strengthening Natura's brand and market presence.

INTERNATIONALIZATION AS A VEHICLE FOR EXPANSION

By as early as 1982 Natura had begun to explore international markets through exports. However, it was not until 1999 the speed of its internationalization in Latin America really gained pace. First Argentina, later Mexico; by 2007 Natura had approximately 100,000 consultants working in Argentina, Mexico, Chile, Peru, Colombia, and Venezuela.

The goal was also to introduce Natura's brand to the European market

'Upside-down' traits:

- Commencing in less developed countries
- Ideological business values
- Direct sales model paired with community-based development
- Intimate innovative relationship to external stakeholders

and to educate the public about the company's unique values. Its first foray was into the Portuguese market in the early 1990s, but this did not result in great success. The venture tempered European ambitions for a while—until 2005 when Natura decided to test its product in the world's most sophisticated center for cosmetics, namely France and specifically Paris. It opened a store in the French capital. Although it did not experience immediate success, Natura's persistence paid off and, after some tweaking to the direct sales model, the French operation started to turn a profit.

Thereafter Natura's organizing principle as far as its international strategy was concerned became: 'Central operations—local adaption.'

THE DRIVE FOR INNOVATION

Product development remained a cornerstone of Natura's business for many years. However, the process of internationalization transformed Natura's innovation process in a major way. R&D, once centered entirely in Cajamar, was decentralized. Collaborations with universities and research centers in other countries (as part of an 'open innovation' strategy) allowed Natura to innovate without high investment (compared to the traditional global players) and to benefit from worldwide innovative capacity.

In 2006, Natura opened a research laboratory in Paris. The company's innovation VP Eduardo Luppi explained that the move was designed to get the company closer to the most advanced techniques in R&D through partnerships with research institutes and European suppliers. Fortuitously it also fueled sales in the French market.

THE CUSTOMERS

An analysis of the players/products in the market revealed the following relationships between consumer value perception and price:[4]

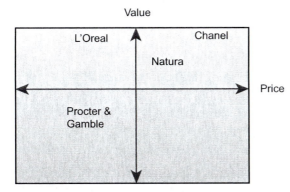

FIGURE 9.1 Natura's Position in the Market

As can be seen from Figure 9.1, Natura is positioned as a brand giving high value but at a premium price (though lower than Chanel's).

ALIGNING WITH STAKEHOLDERS

From 2000 onwards, Natura has used the reporting principles of the Global Reporting Initiative (GRI) to align its social, environmental, and economic progress and reporting. The GRI system is comprehensive and somewhat overwhelming, but by 2006 Natura was able to report on all indicators. This demanded organizational changes and the integration of GRI performance goals with all parts of the organization, including its operating units. In doing this, the company began to understand its three-pronged impact on the bottom line.

The next step was to decide on sustainability goals for the future. Natura defined these through meetings with all kinds of stakeholders and arrived at six priorities, for example 'sustainable development of the Amazon region' and 'education.' The greater challenge, however, was how to evaluate the costs and benefits of these initiatives. For example the company evaluated a policy which involved 30% of all new hires at a distribution center being physically handicapped workers. It was possible to determine the added financial costs of this in the short term, but measuring the gained *value* proved more difficult—not just value to society, but also the value of increased employee morale, long-term productivity, brand etc. For these numbers to be available, Natura would need deeper engagement with stakeholders, who could help provide the required numbers and measures. Today, Natura has involved external stakeholders in panels and discussions as well as deeper community work, and uses the information from stakeholders for planning and product development purposes.

The innovation processes at Natura all involve external stakeholders. Though a network of 'relationships managers', Natura picks up on market issues and trends that it can proactively engage with. Natura has a high innovation rate— approximately 65% of revenues measured over any 24-month period come from new product launches. External partners are also invited into technological innovation processes, and a new social network for scientific partners and institutions, including universities and students. One outcome from these partnerships was the identification of the anti-age benefits of so-called flavonoids in the Brazilian plant Passiflora. This discovery led to a new anti-ageing product range, selling more than 90,000 units in its first six weeks, which was far beyond Natura's own expectations. The most recent initiative in terms of stakeholder-based technology has been the building of a local knowledge and innovation centre, which is under construction in an Amazon region, where local researchers and scientists will work together with Natura to discover even more about Amazon biodiversity.

Such partnerships also provide an interesting additional benefit, namely tax incentives for innovation and promotion. In 2011, these incentives added up to more than USD 5 million in reimbursable and non-reimbursable funding.

CHALLENGE: FINDING THE RIGHT PEOPLE

Natura's high growth rate has demanded a strong recruitment effort across the commercial, operational, and administrative parts of the company. This challenge became even more significant as Natura's plans for internationalization took off.

> The chronic challenge we face when entering a new country is to find the right people. This is our biggest challenge. It is not the lack of talent, it is the fit. Our company is established in our beliefs and we need people fully committed to them, capable of perpetuating them throughout the new organization.[5]

Forums, discussion panels, periodic meetings, and a variety of written material have been used to spread the company's best practices. Throughout the diffusion process, variations on the existing model were developed:

> Natura is not a single model. My responsibility is to ensure processes are uniform, not identical. Processes outside Brazil are subject to variations incorporating local idiosyncrasies. Our beliefs are fully transferred, but cultural details incorporated.[6]

NEXT STEPS

Growth rates for natural cosmetics continue to outperform other categories worldwide. Even in troubled times, growth rates for natural products have continued to outpace most other beauty categories, and the outlook is for this to continue (see Table 9.1).

Whether Natura can continue to capitalize on this trend remains to be seen.

Table 9.1
Natura From the Paradigm Perspective

	Paradigm/ Terminology	Conventional Paradigm	Emerging Paradigm	How does the case illustrate the emerging paradigm?
The innovation dimension	Change mode	Differentiate and value creation	Innovate substantially and impact tactics	65% of revenue comes from new products (over 24 months)
				(Continued)

Table 9.1
(Continued)

	Paradigm/ Terminology	Conventional Paradigm	Emerging Paradigm	How does the case illustrate the emerging paradigm?
The innovation dimension	Size of change	Marginal/ incremental	Revolutionary, unprecedented leaps	Income and product sales double between 2007 and 2011— in the midst of global recession
The innovation dimension	Benchmarking technology	Best practice	Next practice	Relationships with sales consultants and their communities to inform on new products and practices
The cost dimension	Cost structure	Conventional cost structure	Disruptive cost structure	Expansion through 1.4 million well-paid sales consultants. Community-based development
The X-factor dimension	Degree of rationalization	Everything explained/ planned	Focus on exploitation of the X-factor dimension (the unexplained, the unplanned, the unexpected)	Continuously tapping into knowledge from external stakeholders
The regulatory dimension	Regulatory forbearance	Marginally or not addressed	Regulatory game changing	Using partnerships with banks to provide micro-finance for poorer sales consultants, instead of letting their personal debt restrict them
The regulatory dimension	Governmental support	Marginally or not addressed	National subsidies, home market, or cultural advantages	Tax incentives because of partnerships

KEY REFLECTIONS

A. Can we assume that Natura's expansion will continue at the same level of speed and, if so, on what basis?

B. How can the 'relationship approach' be further boosted and accelerated market-wise and innovation-wise?

NOTES

1 In addition to our own research, we have been inspired by the following case studies:

- Eccles, Serafeim, Heffernan 2012: Natura Cosmeticos S.A. Harvard Business School case no. 9–412–052.
- Hashiba 2012: Innovation in Wellbeing.
  A MiX story; one of ten winning entries in the Long-Term Capitalism Challenge 2012 (see http://managementexchange.com/story/innovation-in-well-being)
- World Economic Forum and Boston Consulting Group (2011), Case study: Natura IN: Redefining the Future of Growth: the new sustainability champions. Published by the World Economic Forum.
- Natura: Exporting Brazilian Beauty. Stanford University Case IB 92. 2010.

2 See http://natura.infoinvest.com.br/?language=enu (Corporate and investor site, in English).

3 http://natura.infoinvest.com.br/enu/4036/RelatorioAnual_2011_completo_gri_ingl_html; RelatorioAnual_2011_completo_gri_ingl.html

4 UBS Investment research (2012).

5 Bellona, VP of International Operations, Natura: exporting Brazilian beauty, Stanford Graduate School of Business Case (2012).

6 Daniel Silveira, executive responsible for commercial processes (ibid.).

Chapter 10

Nokia—From Ugly Duckling to White Swan to . . .?

On September 3, 2013 it was announced that Microsoft planned to acquire Nokia. Regulatory approvals are due to take place during 2014. The announcement, the circumstances, and contingencies just galvanize Nokia's end of a life cycle which began as an ugly duckling, gradually developed to a beautiful white swan, but eventually regressed to the position as an ugly duckling again in a fundamentally changed ecosystem now populated by one or more black swans.

> One of the ways in which we've been able to perform better than our competitors is that we're fast to redirect our strategy, if there is a need to.[1]

While Jorma Ollila, Nokia's CEO until 2006, might have some justification for his praise of the company's strategic agility under his own tenure, few would praise Nokia's comparatively low level of strategic agility during and since the take-off of smartphones (from 2007 onwards). In terms of life cycle strategy Nokia makes for an interesting case study, because the company displays such radical variation in strategy and performance over time.

FROM UGLY DUCKLING TO WHITE SWAN

So why do we include Nokia in our study of black swans when its story has not culminated in a sustained high?

There are several factors that justify taking a closer look at some of the inner workings of Nokia's strategy. Firstly, Nokia was an ugly duckling for quite some years as a small conglomerate without any substantial strategic synergies between its different product lines. Nokia's history dates back to 1898 when the company was founded as Finnish Rubber Works, manufacturing rubber boots. Over the years it grew to become an industrial conglomerate with a broad range of disparate core competencies—yet, at this point, there was no strong link with radio or mobile communications.

Nokia's entry into mobile communications was somewhat reluctant, being an attempt to represent Finland as a manufacturer in the pan-Nordic NMT 450 system in the late 1970s/early 1980s. At the time Nokia was neither a market leader, nor a first mover; it still retained businesses in rubber, cables, television, and electronics, too. The upshot was that Nokia was outperformed by Phillips, Ericsson, and Storno when the industry was in its infancy.

This all changed however, when Nokia beefed up its offering during the era of the NMT 900 system, marking its diversification into the business of hand-held mobile devices. It was during the early stages of GSM, from 1987 onwards, that Nokia began to substantially increase its investments as a mobile vendor. Through such investments, the company was able to command an important international position during the initial rollout of GSM networks in the early 1990s.

Nokia also took a very courageous strategic decision—to dispose of its interest in rubber, television, and cables, so that it could focus solely on mobile communications. In so doing, it underwent a transformation from conglomerate to a focused, clean-slate mobile technology firm.

Some industry onlookers appear to have missed the strategic point that Nokia was the first vendor to exploit the full synergies of a dual approach—its high-quality products generated strong demand for Nokia handsets which in turn led to an accelerated demand for additional equipment (often Nokia-based) in the radio networks, and vice versa: building networks with surplus capacity gave mobile operators an incentive to subsidize mobile handsets.

The ugly duckling had transformed itself into a beautiful white swan—at the time, the most beautiful of all!

FROM WHITE SWAN TO BLACK SWAN

Nokia achieved a tremendous feat in revolutionizing the mobile handset business. A large part of this is down to the efforts it made to analyze the way consumers used, or might use, the products—a move which many industry observers have underestimated. This led to the adoption of a lifestyle approach to new enhancements to mobile phones, culminating in the so-called 'feature-rich phone'—comprising camera, memory functions, advanced SMS, watch/alarms, MMS, etc. The focus was to create a richer experience and better life for the mobile customer, not just one based on plain voice telephony. This approach and the subsequent product development proved a tremendous success, creating a market pull far beyond the demand to make and receive plain mobile phone calls.

Nokia's success in the feature-rich mobile handset market is often over-looked today as having represented a big leap by a company. Yet at the time it was huge. Previously, Nokia's product innovation practice had been much more incremental. But suddenly the company came up with something new and disruptive, which offered customers much more than they expected or even realized they needed. By including all of the additional features—camera, alarm, etc.—Nokia was to some extent replacing the need for consumers to carry around separate, single-function devices, thereby creating a new, broader ecosystem for its new product. Consumer surveys began to suggest that people now regarded their mobile handset as being almost on a par with their wallet or credit card—in terms of the perceived impact if they mislaid or lost the device.

Nokia subsequently gained a considerable stronghold as the number two infrastructure vendor—number one in the manufacturing of mobile handsets, with a global market share comfortably surpassing 30% and peaking at the level of 40% (see Table 10.1).

To this point, Nokia's story is a happy one—the transformation of an ugly duckling into a white swan, as the company finally fulfilled its destiny (as a conglomerate, doing quite nicely), and finally a black swan, taking the mobile phone market by storm. By observing and listening to consumers, and executing its vision for the feature phone, Nokia suddenly became the dominant player in the mobile handset market worldwide.

But why didn't this success continue?

Table 10.1
Nokia's Quickly Decreasing Market Share[2]

	2008	2009	2010	2011	2012/Q1	2012/Q2	2012/Q3
Nokia	39.7	36.9	32.6	27.0	20.8	20.6	18.7
Samsung	16.7	19.4	20.1	21.3	23.5	24.1	23.7
Apple	n.s.	n.s.	3.4	6.0	8.8	6.4	6.1
ZTE	n.s.	2.3	3.6	4.3	4.8	4.4	3.1
LG Electronics	8.5	10.1	8.4	5.7	3.4	3.2	3.1
Others	35.1	31.3	31.9	35.7	38.7	41.3	45.3

FROM BLACK SWAN BACK TO UGLY DUCKLING?

Nokia appeared to make a strategic blunder during the evolution of the smartphone—an intelligent, digital device which could send and receive email and browse the internet as well as act as a handy diary/alarm clock/camera.

Initially, Nokia seized this evolving opportunity successfully, gaining an even higher market share of the smartphone sector (39%) in 2009 than its average market share for all mobile devices that same year (36.9%) (see Table 10.1). But in the next wave, something went wrong. From a share of 39% in 2009, Nokia's command of the smartphone market dwindled to under 4% in Q3 of 2012, at which point the company didn't even register among the five largest vendors (see Table 10.2).

Table 10.2
Nokia's Specific Decline in the Smartphone Segment[4]

	2009	2010	2011	2012/Q1	2012/Q2	2012/Q3
Nokia	39.0	33.1	15.7	8.2	6.6	n.s.
Samsung	3.2	7.6	19.1	29.1	32.6	31.3
Apple	14.5	15.7	19.0	24.2	16.9	15.0
Research in Motion	19.9	16.1	10.4	6.7	n.s.	4.3
HTC	4.7	7.1	8.9	4.8	5.7	4.0
Others	18.7	20.4	26.9	27.0	38.2	45.4

It is understandable that a comfortably dominant market position might have slowed Nokia's pulse, causing complacency, but it is difficult to fully explain how Nokia could lose its position so quickly and so dramatically. Even Nokia's CEO, Stephen Elop, seemed puzzled and still somewhat shaken by what happened when asked to comment in early 2011 on the turn of events:

> We fell behind, we missed big trends, and we lost time. At that time we thought we were making the right decisions, but with the benefit of hindsight, we now find ourselves years behind.[3]

Of course the major trigger for Nokia's downfall was Apple's iPhone, which first shipped in 2007, as Elop went on to explain. But how was it that four years later—in 2011, and even into 2012—Nokia still didn't have a handset to rival it?

BIRD STRIKE?

Nokia's undoing was as dramatic as it was rapid. The company's share price plummeted to a tenth of its value—from EUR 27.74 on October 22, 2007 to EUR 2.80 on April 26, 2012 (picking slightly up to around 4 in September of 2013).

In April 2012 Nokia's debt was downgraded to junk status (by Fitch Ratings which lowered Nokia's debt rating to BB+, and gave Nokia a long-term 'negative' outlook, meaning the company is at risk of having its debt downgraded again).

While Nokia still retains a good status in some of the branding indices, there is a declining trend here too. SyncForce ranked Nokia number 2 in 2007, number 5 in 2008, number 6 in 2009, number 20 in 2010 and number 42 in 2011. Interbrand ranked Nokia number 5 in 2007 among its Best Global Brands, a ranking that dropped to 14 in 2011. Prospects for 2012 were not good either, although Nokia clawed back some momentum with the launch of the Lumia 920.

Only time will tell whether Nokia's portfolio of patents and new initiatives (including the Lumia series devices based on Windows 8) are sufficient to keep the company alive with or without helping hands from Microsoft, or whether a black swan (Apple or another unforeseen predator) creates so much destruction for Nokia that it finds itself at a dead end. As Elop has put it:

> Nokia can't just hold these assets and use them as a proprietary way of making its phones better, because people aren't buying the phones.[5]

Can Nokia strike back in time, or is its only future back in the mud room?

Nokia's Downfall

- Nokia was slow to make its mark in the smartphone market and entered with multiple platforms—e.g. Symbian, MeeGo, Windows Mobile.
- By June 2011 Nokia had been overtaken by Apple as the world's biggest smartphone maker by volume.
- Nokia never managed to establish a recognized app store (OVI).
- A strategic blunder saw Nokia blindfolded to the new ecosystems created by Apple and Google.
- Nokia proved inefficient in matching competitors in the low-end market, typically from Southeast Asia.
- Nokia thus became stuck in the middle when attacked by Southeast Asians at the low end and Apple and Android at the high end; its only potential position of strength was serving the emerging markets with 'in-between' terminals.
- Nokia made considerable layoffs during 2011 and 2012.
- Years earlier Nokia's infrastructure department had to merge with Siemens to form Nokia Siemens Networks (NSN). Yet NSN too was losing market strongholds, to not only Ericsson but also newcomers like Huawei.

KEY REFLECTIONS

A. Can a complacent dominant player in an industry broken up by new ecosystems rejuvenate itself? What are Nokia's prospects?

B. If Nokia decides to rejuvenate its strategy (other than the alliance with Microsoft set out in 2010/2011), how can it protect itself against the future impact of black swans?

C. What should we make of the following quote from Elop? "We have a lot of work ahead. We know that we are bringing a beautiful product to the market. The Lumia 920 has gotten fantastic reviews, but now we have to translate that into sales results."

D. Finally, what are the prospects of Nokia's devices being acquired and integrated into the Microsoft organization?

NOTES

1 Jorma Ollila 1999 (*CNN Money*, 12 October) (http://money.cnn.com/1999/10/12/technology/tel99_nokia/).
2 IDC Worldwide Mobile Phone Trackers and Merrill Lynch Research.
3 Stephen Elop 2011 (from Elop's leaked memo disseminated to employees in February 2011), following his appointment as CEO of Nokia, see Microsoft employees should get ready to plunge 30 meters into the freezing cold waters of the North Sea, by Matthew Yglesias, posted September 3, 2013 at Slate Magazine (blog).
4 IDC Worldwide Mobile Phone Trackers and Merrill Lynch Research.
5 See www.newsfactor.com, November 16, 2012.

Chapter 11

Ryanair—a True Disruptor

As we saw in the case of Emirates, Ryanair has also made its assault on the airline industry from a non-traditional location, this time Ireland—isolated, sparsely populated, and historically submissive to the UK. However the Ryanair case also breaks fundamentally with conventional thinking—introducing aggressive discounts to the market. Ryanair's dual-pronged strategy, then, has been to take a cost leader position as well as invoking a differentiator strategy—inventing a new type of disruptive strategy at the same time.

BECOMING A NEW KID ON THE BLOCK

Ryanair was established by the Ryan family in 1985 with a share capital of just GBP 1. The first service launched that July, on a 15-seater Bandeirante aircraft, flying daily from Waterford in the southeast of Ireland to London Gatwick. The number of passengers annually was 5,000.

After three years of rapid growth in its fleet and routes and following intense price competition with Aer Lingus and British Airways, Ryanair accumulated GBP 20m. in losses and underwent a substantial restructuring. The Ryan family invested a further GBP 20m. in the company, and copying the low-fares model favored by Southwest Airlines in the US, the airline was relaunched under new management as Europe's first low-fares airline with a "No frills, low cost" mantra. Ryanair was now offering the lowest fares in each of its target markets and high-frequency flights; it moved to a single aircraft fleet type, scrapped free drinks and expensive meals on board, and slashed its lowest fares from GBP 99 to just GBP 59 return. Its annual passenger throughput rose to 745,000.

In 1997 Ryanair became a public company, following a successful flotation on the Dublin and NASDAQ (New York) Stock Exchanges. Its shares were oversubscribed by a factor of more than 20 and the share price surged from a flotation price of EUR 11 to close at EUR 25.5 on the first day of trading. All Ryanair employees received shares as part of the flotation process and at the close of the first day's trading, they were together sitting on more than EUR 100 million worth of stock. Passenger numbers by now had soared to 3,730,000 a year.

Since then, Ryanair has continued to open up new routes in Europe. In July 1998 new shares were issued to raise over GBP 110m. to help pay for additional aircraft. Ryanair was voted 'Airline of the Year' by the Irish Air Transport Users Committee, and the 'Best Managed National Airline' in the world by the prestigious *International Aviation Week* magazine. A further million passengers switched their allegiance to the company.

Aggressively low fares, already the backbone of the company, were seen as key to the airline's success. CEO Michael O'Leary believed they could go even lower, commenting:

> I don't see why in 10 years' time you wouldn't fly people for free. Why don't airports pay us for delivering the passengers to their shops?[1]

Where traditional business logic would point to minimum fares being essential to cover the high costs of running a large air fleet, Ryanair has turned this thinking on its head.

In 2010, the airline's traffic grew by 8% to 73 million passengers, with the average fare at just EUR 39 and no fuel surcharges for customers, despite a sharp increase in fuel costs. Ryanair took delivery of a further 40 new aircraft as the fleet rose to 272 Boeing 737–800s. The total staff by now was around 9,000 people.

For Ryanair, bold enough to challenge accepted norms, the sky appears to be the limit. In 2012 the airline transported 79.3 million passengers (a further 5% growth) and turned a profit of EUR 569 (an increase of 13% from 2011). Some 200 new routes were opened to give Ryanair 1,600 destinations on its flight map.

Ryanair's strategy is at odds with traditional thinking, but so too are its profits at odds with the performance of the airline's competitors. In an ever more brutally competitive market, Ryanair keeps growing and thriving. It continues to challenge and innovate too—continually inventing new ideas for lowering the price through, for example, upright passage—a real provocation in the airline industry where for safety and comfort's sake passengers have always had to be seated. As O'Leary puts it:

> I'd love to operate aircraft where we take out the back 10 rows and put in hand rails. We'd say if you want to stand, it's EUR 5. People say: "Oh but the people standing may get killed if there's a crash." Well, with respect, the people sitting down might get killed as well.[2]

Michael O'Leary is still the CEO of the company (although he has long declared his intention to step down). Ryanair is still successful, but is being attacked more aggressively by other carriers. Among other challenges Ryanair is being accused of taking risks—by flying with the minimum allowance of fuel to cut down on flight costs. So, even this deeply ambitious black swan may be reaching its limits.

A LEADING DISRUPTOR!

Ryanair has revolutionized the airline industry over the last twenty years. From being an ugly duckling, it has developed into an unapologetic, aggressive black swan as it has set new standards for how an airline can work. Very few people could have foreseen a day when airline tickets might be given away for free, or when a round trip from London to Stockholm might cost less than EUR 50.

But how was Ryanair able to achieve this position as an industry disruptor?

The 'no frills, low cost' strategy is central to the airline's vision. This has

> The list of counterintuitive ideas is long:
>
> - Flight tickets for free.
> - Secondary airports.
> - Only one flight type.
> - Positive interest in entertaining court cases.
> - Aggressive on certain environmental issues.
> - Contracting staff in some cases without salary or salary paid out in low-tax countries.

been the backbone and the managerial mantra of Ryanair's business model since it decided on the discount strategy. Ryanair has undoubtedly been inspired by Southwest Airlines in the US—a company started in 1971 which has grown to become the most successful low-cost carrier in North America.

However, even though the two companies are operating from the same philosophy and the same type of cost base, they are managed in quite different ways. Where Ryanair can be thought of as the 'naughty boy' in the class, Southwest's image is more that of the 'nice girl.' For example, Ryanair conducts aggressive and political mass marketing. Very often it is quite provocative. The company also exploits media lawsuits for publicity purposes, rather than launching very expensive advertising campaigns.

Ryanair's aggression is also evident in its repeated attempts to acquire the Irish national carrier Aer Lingus. As O'Leary put it:

> The proposed merger of Ryanair and Aer Lingus will form one Irish airline group with the financial strength to compete with Europe's 3 major airline groups—Air France, British Airways and Lufthansa.[3]

Ryanair has been doggedly determined to acquire its rival since 2006 but its advances have been rejected by the Irish authorities and the EU Commission which have argued that the suggested merger would kill off competition and undermine consumer choice.

Other aggressive moves have included:

- Productivity-based compensation schemes—all compensation being related to performance.
- Outsourcing to third parties—third-party contractors are used in all airports.
- Reorganization of sales and distribution—all sales are done electronically (there are no expensive agents).
- Harmonizing and scrutinizing the fleet—Ryanair uses only one type of plane in its fleet (Boeing), giving it much greater flexibility as staff can be moved around with ease.
- Utilization—the airline has the lowest turnaround rates in the industry, helped by its planes making full use of entrances and exits at both ends.
- Rethinking the classic customer care program (reverse caring?)—low prices, punctuality, and efficient and uncrowded airports.
- Utilizing remote airports—increasing business in these airports and using them at a very low cost; even encouraging the airports to pay to have Ryanair land there.
- Aggressive negotiations with airline authorities—continually trying to push the boundaries.
- Advanced used of technology—Ryanair was a first mover within electronic ticketing.
- Employees—apparently Ryanair does not find it difficult to recruit, even though the airline has a strict personnel policy
- Leadership—using the CEO's controversial stances to capture the headlines in the press and create buzz across the airline industry
- Fighting the unions—rather than shying away from trouble, Ryanair is always ready to take on new battles
- Environmental position—low CO_2 emissions (a positive side effect of its brutal cost-cutting!).

Even though Ryanair has been very successful the company is also widely criticized for its attitude and way of doing business. But O'Leary welcomes any publicity as good publicity, famously saying:

> One of the weaknesses of the company now is it is a bit cheap and cheerful and overly nasty, and that reflects my personality.[4]

Although often in the firing line, Michael O'Leary's success is widely acknowledged by his peers, as is reflected in the comments by the chairman of BMI British Midland:

> He is almost certainly one of the most successful leaders in the industry, with a unique business model, discipline and an extraordinary level of confidence.[5]

FUTURE OUTLOOK

It is hard to argue with the runaway success of Ryanair, thanks to its consistent and very aggressive discount strategy. Thanks to its boldness, the company has achieved many of its goals in both customer and financial terms.

Even though competition in the low-cost market has grown even stronger, plenty of opportunities appear to remain for more/new attacks. Indeed, Ryanair seems to have the elements needed to further develop its business in the future: a good product delivered at a remarkably low cost, better service perception, a recognized and highly valued brand, customer support and lean technology with easy ordering, ticketing, quick boarding, and high turnaround rates.

So far Ryanair continues to operate only in Europe. However, other low-cost carriers such as Norwegian are about to open up transatlantic routes. It remains to be seen whether Ryanair will stick to its present market or whether it will be lured by the promise of new and bigger opportunities overseas. Will this great black swan cross the pond?

Table 11.1
Ryanair from the Paradigm Perspective

	Paradigm/ terminology	Conventional Paradigm	Emerging Paradigm	How does the case illustrate the emerging paradigm?
The surprise dimension	Starting block	First mover, pole position, and sustainable advantages	Late or last or unexpected mover and ephemeral advantages	Untraditional moves for a low-cost carrier. Focus on items incumbents keep away from (service, comfort in flights, remote airports, emission, court cases, etc.)
The innovation dimension	Change mode	Differentiate and value creation	Innovate substantially and impact tactics	Selected innovations (electronic ticketing, 'upright seating' potentially) and destroying value and creating value instantly

The innovation dimension	Benchmarking technology	Best practice	Next practice	Standardizing technology (harmonizing fleet). Low cost not only by cutting cost but also by generating revenues from alternative sources (rental companies, airports, hotels, etc.)
The X-factor dimension	Degree of rationalization	Everything explained/planned	Focus on exploitation of the X factor (the unexplained, the unplanned, the unexpected)	X factor = embedded in the CEO Michael O'Leary with his consistent focus on a disruptive business model
The regulatory dimension	Market perfection	Market forces	Regulatory distortions/wins	Often wins the media war on regulatory matters (even when losing cases (e.g. its proposed acquisition of Aer Lingus))

KEY REFLECTIONS

A. Ryanair has been very successful for many years. However, the competition has become stronger and the market even more transparent—will Ryanair need to reinvent its business model or can the company maintain a black swan position (as disrupter of the airline industry)?

B. Succession: Ryanair's achievements are inextricably linked with the provocative and aggressively ambitious individual, Michael O'Leary. Even though replacement is always possible, what will happen with Ryanair when a new CEO takes over?

NOTES

1 *Daily Telegraph*, 5 September, 2012.
2 *Irish Examiner*, September 8, 2012 (www.irishexaminer.com/ireland/michael-olearys-plane-speaking-touches-down-on-passengers-206849.html).
3 *Daily Telegraph*, September 5, 2013.
4 Ibid.
5 Sir Michael Bishop, chairman, BMI British Midland (see www.theguardian.com/business/2002/jun/16/theairlineindustry.theobserver).

Chapter 12

Tata Motors—Reverse Imperialism

FROM LOCAL TO GLOBAL CONGLOMERATE

Tata is to all intents and purposes an India-based company, which has built up a considerable part of its strength by working with a diversified product portfolio locally on the subcontinent for many years. That Tata is now rapidly transforming itself into a global conglomerate seems impressive in this context. Today, the group has 450,000 employees and revenues approaching USD 100 billion. An 800% growth in revenues from 2002 to 2011 might be enough to qualify Tata as a corporate black swan, galvanized by the fact that it is now one of the largest business entities in the world. The group today is made up of more than 100 active companies, of which six globally are among the 10 largest in their industry; four are in the top three.

This is deliberate on Tata's part. As group chairman Ratan Tata once put it:

> At Tata, we believe that if we are not among the top three in an industry, we should look seriously at what it would take to become one of the top three players . . . or think about exiting the industry.[1]

In its emerging capacity as a global conglomerate, Tata has also become the largest donor in the history of Harvard Business School thanks to its support for a USD 50 million building, 'Tata Hall', in Boston in the US—a gift that would have been unthinkable if the business had continued down its initial road as a local Indian company.

Notwithstanding the fact that Tata is hugely interesting at the corporate level with its diversified conglomerate approach, we have chosen to focus on the case of just one arm of the conglomerate, namely Tata Motors.

TATA MOTORS—FROM A DEVELOPING COUNTRY TO A DEVELOPED COUNTRY AND BACK AGAIN!

Tata Motors was founded in 1987 to focus on the automotive industry—initially in India where it brought to market the first ignition-operated car in 1998. Its core product lines are cars, buses, and trucks. Although India was the target market for many years, the company has now begun to make good progress in establishing a foothold outside of its home country, through a series of strategic acquisitions.

Today, Tata is one of the world's larger car makers—number 3 in bus manufacturing and number 4 within medium/heavy CVs. But now the company is displaying ambitions to become even more prominent on the global scene. In 2008/2009 it caused a stir by unveiling the so-called Nano car at the startlingly cheap price point of USD 2,000. Initially, the product enjoyed only limited success with just 70,000 units sold annually. The car is positioned to take a share of the market for new cars sold for use in emerging countries; it is not designed for the US and European markets which demand more equipment and drivability, and where the regulations on crash testing and emissions are also more stringent (that is not to say that a more advanced Nano couldn't one day take a large bite out of the car market in developed countries . . .).

On a global scale, the c.800 million cars sold in 2012 is expected to grow to two billion cars in just a few years, pointing to a vast market opportunity as more consumers in emerging markets take to the road. It is not surprising then that Tata Motors is working hard to develop offerings at the low end of the market in order to command a lion's share of this attractive growth, which will be concentrated in these previously under-served markets. In the meantime sales of new cars in established markets such as Europe are in decline. Yet, for now, conventional car makers persist in focusing their energies on these more mature markets—perhaps because it is what they've always done. In identifying the source of potential new growth, Tata would seem to be ahead of the game.

TATA'S ACQUISITION OF JAGUAR LAND ROVER

In fact, Tata is full of surprises. A major one was the unforeseen acquisition of Jaguar/Land Rover, two British car icons, in 2008. Making a huge splash in the market, this strategic acquisition brought iconic brands to the Tata portfolio and boosted Tata Motor's profile

The Jaguar Land Rover Deal

- Tata acquired 100% of the shares in Jaguar Land Rover (JLR) in 2008 for USD 2.3 billion. The company was turned around under Tata, after it was overnight. Moreover, it was the first major tactical step in executing the company's cross-border strategy. This has proved highly successful—from 2011 on, Jaguar Land Rover has sold more units in China than in the original home market, the UK. Group CEO Ratan Tata explains his thought process:

> At no stage should [Jaguar Land Rover] be conceived of as a Mondeo in another garb. The company has been thinking along those lines. It hasn't been, "How can we get a car to sell 400,000?" It has been, "Can we create an entry-level car that is a Jaguar?"[2]

- rejected financial assistance from the UK Labour government.
- JLR generated profits between 2009 and 2012 worth a higher aggregate value than the acquisition price.
- The car production has been expanded considerably since the takeover, reaching 243,621 cars by March 31, 2011. In March 2012, JLR reported its best month with more than 45,000 cars sold. Insiders believe that the company will soon deliver 500,000 cars annually.
- From 2012 onwards JLR is expanding with new factories in Wolverhampton in the UK, and in China.
- In 2012 JLR was valued at USD 20 billion, i.e. almost 9 times the purchase price in 2008.

REVERSE IMPERIALISM

So what led an Indian business group to set its sights on British assets? Tata Motor had been successful in its Indian home market but faced a serious challenge in the global market. Its move to acquire British icons allows a strategy of combining low-end brands (in India) with high-end iconic brands (like Jaguar Land Rover).

The JLR acquisition offers benefits not only at the high end but also at the low end of the market. Moreover, with the increased prestige and the increased brand value introduced by Jaguar Land Rover, there is now a serious opportunity for Tata to gain momentum in the mid-market too. (The first step in this plan has been to mix in mid

Tata Group—on the Acquisition Trail

- Tetley was acquired by Tata in 2000, helping Tata become the largest tea-maker in the world (Tetley is the most bought tea brand in the UK).
- Anglo-Dutch Steel was acquired by Tata in 2007 for USD 12.11 billion, the biggest overseas acquisition by an Indian company.
- Tata Chemicals acquired the leading vacuum salt producer British Salt in 2010.
- Tata Consultancy Services has taken over a considerable number of high-profile IT contracts from UK vendors in the UK.
- Tata pitched for the acquisition of Cable & Wireless Worldwide in

market, strategies through an alliance with Fiat Chrysler.)

If this kind of 'reverse imperialism' continues to pay off, Ratan Tata's comments below become even more poignant:

> April 2012 but was unsuccessful this time (Vodafone took the deal).
>
> ■ Indian Tata continues to look for opportunities to acquire crown jewels among UK firms—who will be next?

> I don't believe in taking right decisions. I take decisions and then make them right.[3]

The upshot is that Tata Motors is now quickly approaching near market leadership, or at least reaching a par with some of the largest car makers in the automotive industry.

TATA AND THE EMERGING PARADIGM

Tata has employed reverse imperialism as part of a deliberate strategy to surprise the market, as we have seen through the sudden and unexpected takeover of iconic brands such as Jaguar Land Rover. These moves bear all the hallmarks of black swan behavior—the surprise of the Jaguar Land Rover takeover, the unexpected turnaround of a failing company by an Indian parent company, and the unpredicted cross-segment, cross-country success Tata has gone on to champion with these world-famous brands.

Table 12.1
Tata Motor from the Paradigm Perspective

	Paradigm/ terminology	Conventional Paradigm	Emerging Paradigm	How does the case illustrate the emerging paradigm?
The surprise dimension	Market position	Market leadership	Zero market share = perfect start	As a conglomerate in a BRIC country gaining strength to make surprising foreign investments

The innovation dimension	Change mode	Differentiate & value creation	Innovate substantially & Impact tactics	Instead of bringing out the usual mass-market cars, Tata Motors attacks from both the high end (via JLR) and the low end (with the Nano)
The X-factor dimension	Degree of rationalization	Everything explained/ planned	Focus on exploitation of the X factor (the unexplained, the unplanned, the unexpected)	Reverse imperialism—a company in an emerging economy takes over iconic brands in developed countries and makes these further profitable by satisfying undiscovered demand in emerging countries

KEY REFLECTIONS

A. Will reverse imperialism or something like it become key to understanding the strategies and plans of companies in emerging economies that were not born global?

B. The Tata Motors case prompts the question how can an Indian company with no insight into British/Western luxury brands turn around JLR so successfully in such a short time—especially when the British owners and the British government had given up?

C. Given Tata's success in the low end and high end of the market, what are its prospects for success in the mid-market?

NOTES

1 Ratan Tata (November 2001) (We need a consortium of like-minded companies to face the multinationals, interview with Ratan Tata, *Outlook Magazine*).
2 Ratan Tata (October 2012) (Jaguar/Landrover to add models, stay true to heritage, an interview with Ratan Tata by Diana T. Kurylko, *Automotive News Europe*).
3 Ratan Tata (May 2012) (see the portrait of Ratan Tata, *Economic Times*, May 25, 2012). Nokia was slow to make its mark in the smartphone market and entered with multiple platforms—e.g. Symbian, MeeGo, Windows Mobile.

Part III

Beyond Strategy and Metrics

Chapter 13

Going Beyond Strategy

As Rita Gunther McGrath, a professor at Columbia Business School in New York, rightly pointed out in June 2013, "strategy is stuck." But maybe strategy is more than just stuck, and perhaps this is for more reasons than McGrath has acknowledged.[1]

We have witnessed endless competition within the conventional paradigm, as management gurus have sought to pinpoint the ultimate recipe for company success—the recipe for producing gold, as we have characterized it. Over time the number of proposed recipes has multiplied—some of these simpler, others slightly more complex through the inclusion of additional rules.

The 'iron triangle' between MBAs, CEOs, and consultants has kept the recipe business alive. When a recipe was incorporated within an MBA program, this resulted in the given formula moving out with candidates into the workplace to the point that these (future MBA) CEOs advised by MBA consultants would take this common body of knowledge and put it into practice in real-world projects. Any subsequent failure of the recipe to deliver the desired results could either be disguised as success based on halo techniques,[2] or lead to repair through the application of another recipe. In this way, the cookbook business has been perpetuated for decades.

In a more complex, cyclical, and globalized world, the gap between the conventional paradigm and companies' real-life contingencies has become overstretched. To close this gap, we need to go *beyond* strategy and start afresh. The numerous cases of success by black swan companies, as outlined throughout this book, provide startling evidence that the biggest successes today often come when businesses have torn up the conventional cookbook and are bold enough to buck every accepted norm and trend. What most black swan companies have in common is that they are acting in direct *contrast* to the recommendations set out by the conventional paradigm.

In the sections below we will venture a bit further beyond these findings.

At the beginning of this book, we asked whether the unpredictable can be predicted. Later, we discussed the dichotomy between what is known and what is unknown, looking at how business leaders' mindsets and company strategies are formed around these notions (most commonly the former). Given what we now know about black swan companies, let us now revisit the idea of knowns and unknowns as a way of rounding off our journey.

Conventional strategy thinking deals very much with what is known. This is obvious from an analytical point of view—whenever analytical tools are used to beef up the knowledge in strategy processes, such as SWOT, VRIO, the Boston Matrix, the GE/McKinsey Matrix, the Strategy Canvas, etc. It is equally obvious from reading the cookbook literature, as the recipes here are all based on well-known factors/accepted truths. However, in many cases these elements are either used to sustain solutions (e.g. in the form of 'best practice') or to extend the solution in a linear way.

The conventional paradigm deals with only part of this known universe. That is, strategy 'cookbooks' would still have many shortcomings even if the world comprised only the known universe. As many of the proposed recipes are based on interviews with CEOs, we must take the halo effect into account. This suggests that some successes are 'oversold'—i.e. that failures are disguised so that the company in question emerges as triumphant (at least as long as the CEO interview takes place during their tenure!). Another distortion within the universe of 'known knowns' is the fact that recipes derived from one company in one specific industry or context are often generalized to be valid for all other companies. This is despite the fact that experience shows that it is difficult—in many instances impossible—to transfer management and strategy best practice across companies and industries, not to mention countries.

However, there are also known 'unknowns' to consider, i.e. the things we *know* we don't know. It is dangerous to assume that past success is an indicator of future success, especially today when markets move so quickly. Yet this is an assumption that is often made, and one that is encouraged by traditional strategy literature and management practice—for example through the emphasis placed on 'known best practice.' Senior decision makers would give their organizations a far better chance if they were also able to consider and address the as yet largely unknown 'next' practice. As we explored in Chapter 5, Apple, under Steve Jobs, provided an excellent example of a company that worked hard to turn unknowns into knowns—to look beyond current best practice and define *next* practice, and then to keep this to itself—by building a high wall around the resulting innovation, so that Apple's breakthrough discovery would remain unknown to the outside world for as long as possible.

But there are also developments that are impossible to predict: unknowns that cannot be foreseen—blind spots or *'unknown* unknowns.' The things we don't know we don't know. Looking back over the black swan examples cited in Chapters 5–12, we might be left with the following questions as we try to assess the importance of 'unknown unknowns':

- Wouldn't Nokia, Siemens, Sony, Ericsson, HTC, and many other (formerly) successful producers of also high-end mobile handsets have fared differently if they, in time, had understood and fully appreciated the mindset, culture, and resulting success generated by Apple?

- Might Eastman Kodak have been able to avoid filing for bankruptcy in 2012 if it had succeeded in transforming its portfolio of 1,100 digital imaging patents into business? It seems surprising that one of America's most acclaimed companies, a pioneer in establishing the market for camera film before going on to dominate the field for more than 125 years, was not capable of capitalizing on new, advanced technology which it already had in-house?

- Might the main national airlines have been able to plan successful pre-emptive moves if they had been able to anticipate the success of discount carriers like Ryanair, or the ambitious intercontinental strike by Emirates which has challenged the entire way international routes are configured?

- How was it that a Chinese telecoms equipment manufacturer was able to come seemingly from nowhere to become number one in such a large global market? Ericsson, NSN, Motorola, Nortel, Alcatel, and others were caught by surprise, and too late to do anything about it, failing in both their analysis of what was happening and in their ability to adjust their own mindsets. But why?

- What does it tell us about the mindset and strategies of established British companies that an Indian group (Tata) was able to sweep in without warning and acquire—and turnaround—ailing businesses that were once considered the national crown jewels? Jewels that even the biggest British powers had been unable to restore to their former glory. Could it be that they were held back by outmoded ways of thinking, while fresh eyes could see a different future for the companies?

- Staying with the theme of emerging economies, who would have thought that cataract surgery could be executed professionally for free or for as little as USD 18 in India? Or that a Latin American company championing community based development could beat Western cosmetics giants in terms of growth, innovation, and profitability?

These observations highlight the importance of being aware of and prepared for the emergence of unknown forces and behaviors. This applies both to companies acting knowingly and consciously in the unknown universe (like Apple, Huawei, Tata, Ryanair, and others) and companies which until now have restricted their vision and mindset to the known universe (for example Nokia, Ericsson, Motorola, Alcatel, Nortel, Kodak, Jaguar, Tetley, Sabena, Swissair, and many others).

Table 13.1 on the next page summarizes some important distinctions between the unknown and the known, and between external recognition and one's own

Table 13.1
The Strategic Windows of Black Swan Companies[3]

		External Recognition			
		Known			**Unknown**
Own	**Unknown**	Unknown/Known	2	3	Unknown/Unknown
Mindest	**Known**	Known/Known	1	4	Known/Unknown

mindset. It leaves the possibility that, as long as established companies are blind to unforeseen possibilities and the influence of forces outside of their experience, they are inadvertently leaving a window open for competitors. Each of the four 'windows' (quadrants) will be addressed in turn.

Where the conventional strategy is largely accounted for within the known-known universe, as represented in quadrant 1 in Table 13.1, the focus of this book has been to explore the new unknown universe of the remaining three quadrants. That is why we talk about moving 'beyond strategy'—by this we mean both passing the frontier of conventional strategy, and investigating the inner workings of strategy in the unknown universe. In order to craft a comprehensive strategy, we also need to be open to what is unknown.

In quadrant 2 we see an agile and open mindset which recognizes that there are unknowns out there. As we saw in the case of Ryanair, the company devised the notion of free tickets without knowing whether this was a sustainable strategy. The airline also learned, possibly without having considered the possibility previously, that becoming embroiled in court cases contributed positively to its core strategy—even if the outcome was to lose the case. To traditional strategy advisers this might have seemed counterintuitive, but Ryanair has made its name by being bold, even arrogant enough, to ignore what others think, and to reject accepted wisdom. Explaining this in terms of Table 13.1, the company knowingly moved from quadrant 1 to quadrant 2 based on its aggressive and explorative mindset, which enabled it to open up and exploit blind spots.

Quadrant 4 indicates the opposite trend. Here, the company is (fully) aware of new strategic opportunities and is able to colonize from external sources. Huawei is a case in point here. It diligently and quickly migrated from 2G to 3G and 'suddenly' became market leader in 4G too—the latest advance in mobile communications allowing true mobile broadband services. One of its tactics was to colonize a number of intellectual property rights. This went hand in hand with Huawei's strategy of 'countryside surrounding cities': Huawei deliberately targeted operators in the least developed countries to build ground cover, as a means by which to later conquer competitors in their own home markets. In this way Huawei managed to convert opportunities into 'transient advantages' (a term coined by McGrath).[4]

Finally, quadrant 3 is the most curious,[5] being completely empty for many companies and disregarded in conventional strategic theory. However, the case of Apple shows that companies are able to tap into even this inner part of the unknown universe. Under Steve Jobs, Apple managed to develop products, most prominently the iPhone, that went far beyond the initial vision of how far innovation could go. In the process it successfully colonized its new, broader environment to an extreme extent. The case of Emirates is similar in that the airline could not have anticipated the full implication of its Dubai location. Likewise Tata could not have anticipated in 2009 that China could become the largest market for Jaguar Land Rover cars.

For Apple in particular, but also for a number of other companies, working with the unknown universe can create an immense Return on Strategy.[6]

Our research revealed that something all black swan companies have in common is that they are operating efficiently and effectively within the universe of the unknowns, proactively trying to push the limits towards the unknowns with often immediate impact.

This can be thought of on a sliding scale, as depicted in Figure 13.1.

Figure 13.1 is a development of Table 13.1, this time presenting the four quadrants on a sliding scale. It also highlights the extent to which the conventional paradigm fails to take account of the wider universe. Appendix 1 further expands on how we are using this toolkit in the context of black swan strategies.

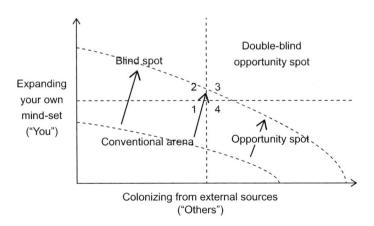

FIGURE 13.1 The Toolkit from which to Develop a Strategy Based on Unknowns

CONVENTIONAL STRATEGY, CONVENTIONAL PARADIGM

As we discussed in Chapter 2, the conventional paradigm relies heavily on prescriptive recipes: the assumption that simply following a cookbook will help companies achieve so much that they eventually, by default, emerge as white swans.

There is ample evidence that companies run a great risk by putting strategy on autopilot. For a number of reasons, the expected successes of many companies never materialize or quickly wither away. Generally speaking this is because the conventional paradigm, in all its various guises, fails to cater for all eventualities, focusing as it does on the knowns and not the unknowns, and placing too much store by past achievements.

More specific characteristics of the conventional paradigm are set out in Table 13.2.

Generally, the five dimensions addressed to characterize the conventional paradigm paint a picture of a 'pure' market economy without substantial distortions. It assumes the ability of a company to diligently work out a strategy process in which proper analyses and a mindset attuned to the received rules will transform the ugly duckling into a beautiful white swan. This is what we

Table 13.2
Recapping the Essence of the Conventional Paradigm

	Paradigm/Terminology	Conventional Paradigm
The surprise dimension	Market position	Market leadership
The surprise dimension	Starting block	First mover, pole position, and sustainable advantages
The innovation dimension	Change mode	Differentiate and value creation
The innovation dimension	Size of change	Marginal/incremental
The innovation dimension	Benchmarking technology	Best practice
The innovation dimension	Methodology	Analytical
The cost dimension	Cost structure	Conventional cost structure
The X-factor dimension	Degree of rationalization	Everything explained/planned
The regulatory dimension	Market perfection	Market forces
The regulatory dimension	Regulatory forbearance	Marginally or not addressed
The regulatory dimension	Governmental support	Marginally or not addressed

saw in quadrant 1 of Table 13.1, where companies are operating on the basis of known factors, and in which there is no mental space left for any significant unknowns.

If we move to an even more specific level, many companies working within this universe adhere to a very strict quantitative understanding and execution. This is often represented by the Balanced Score Card approach and subsequent use of key performance indicators (KPIs) throughout the company.

Yet again, this is part of a *Mediocristan* where most things are calculated according to a mean and what is already known.

THE EMERGING PARADIGM

In sharp contrast to what we have learnt about the conventional paradigm are traits from the emerging paradigm. The mindset and analytical approach here is in such a way that the future erupts without following any defined existing/known logic; this paradigm explicitly addresses what is (as yet) unknown. This places focus on extreme events, unforeseen contingencies, sudden opportunities, etc.

Some of the main characteristics of the emerging paradigm are summarized in more specific terms in Table 13.3.

In the following pages, we will address each of the five dimensions depicted in Table 13.3 as characterizing the emerging paradigm.

The surprise dimension breaks with the traditional Michael Porter-based thinking on how to gain competitive advantage. Having market leadership is by no means an advantage, nor is a first mover position, when up against black swan competition. Unfortunately, there is not very much theory developed around the surprise dimension but empirically we have some strong evidence. Consider how established market players including Nokia, Alcatel, Motorola, many national airlines, and distinguished UK brands have been caught out by the unexpected moves of Apple, Huawei, Ryanair, Emirates, and Tata.

One of the most striking examples of all is that of Indian group Tata and its swift, surprise acquisitions of some iconic UK brands. Not only was Tata Motors' acquisition of Jaguar Land Rover unexpected in its own right, it resulted in probably the fastest turnaround seen in the automotive industry; in next to no time, Tata made the acquired company hugely profitable in the same factories that had turned in massive losses under previous ownership.

Then there is the way Apple has orchestrated some of its product launches. Standard operating procedure for a company would be to make pre-launches, to show up at the annual 80,000-delegate Mobile World Congress, and to inform and cultivate the stakeholders. But not at Apple. Apple tore up the textbook and deliberately built Chinese walls, displayed seemingly demotivating and

Table 13.3
The Essence of the Emerging Paradigm Summarized

	Paradigm/ Terminology	Conventional Paradigm	Emerging Paradigm
The surprise dimension	Market position	Market leadership	Zero market share = perfect start
The surprise dimension	Starting block	First mover, pole position, and sustainable advantages	Late or last or unexpected mover and ephemeral advantages
The innovation dimension	Change mode	Differentiate and value creation	Innovate substantially and impact tactics
The innovation dimension	Size of change	Marginal/incremental	Revolutionary, unprecedented leaps
The innovation dimension	Benchmarking technology	Best practice	Next practice
The innovation dimension	Methodology	Analytical	Passionate
The cost dimension	Cost structure	Conventional cost structure	Disruptive cost structure
The X-factor dimension	Degree of rationalization	Everything explained/ planned	Focus on exploitation of the X-dimension (the unexplained, the unplanned, the unexpected)
The regulatory dimension	Market perfection	Market forces	Regulatory distortions/ wins
The regulatory dimension	Regulatory forbearance	Marginally or not addressed	Regulatory game changing
The regulatory dimension	Governmental support	Marginally or not addressed	National subsidies, home market, or cultural advantages

threatening behavior towards core employees, allowing no one other than Steve Jobs to have a full overview and a share of the passion. But if it had followed the cookbook it is very unlikely it would have achieved anything like the success the iPhone has enjoyed.

The innovation dimension also highlights considerable difference between the two paradigms. Drawing on conventional wisdom, Porter taught companies that differentiation is a very viable strategy when you wish to innovate. Often this would be a piecemeal process, a common approach being to execute strategy by benchmarking against 'best practice.' But again this means operating on the basis of what is known or what can be made known. In the *emerging* paradigm, black swan companies paddle furiously upstream to enter unchartered waters, determined *not* to adhere to the best practice of others, but rather to create a new practice. Belonging to the unknown universe, and giving no clue to their plans, these players constitute a very real threat to today's incumbents.

It is how Huawei in China was able to sneak up on its rivals under the radar. For some years the company had been grossly underestimated by its peers. But it played its hand very cleverly when it came to innovation. First of all, it chose to base its product line solely on IP technology long before its competitors (giving it the advantage of being the last mover, unfettered by old legacy technology). Second, it took a very aggressive approach to patenting, registering a staggering 40,000 of these in the space of a few years. Third, Huawei knew that the final battle would take place in the 4G mobile field when cellular mobile would begin to conquer the broadband market traditionally served by the fixed network. So successful were its achievements here that the company even managed to take on former market leader Ericsson in its home market of Scandinavia.

The cost dimension is interesting, too. Conventional business-school thinking is that companies need to price their products and services according to average costs. For incumbents, monopolists, utilities, and the public sector this has often led to a strange mechanism according to which the company or institution seeks full cost coverage by setting prices according to the existing/old cost base, taking sunk costs into account. In the case of private companies, there is then a profit on top. This model is very predictable, given that historic and present costs are well known. Black swans reject these norms, willing to plunge courageously into the unknown world of future costs. If they set prices lower than expected by core consumers, customers will begin purchasing and/or purchase more. This may further accelerate the downward trend of marginal cost, often approaching zero, whereby a disruptive cost structure emerges.

We have seen this 'Freemium' approach taken by the likes of Skype, Google, Facebook, Ryanair, and many others. By pricing the products at zero or a very low level, these companies have been able to stimulate high demand, and capture a large customer base, paving the way for reverse revenue streams from third parties, and/or an opportunity to promote additional products and services. At the other extreme, companies such as Apple and Emirates have found that customers are willing to pay a premium because of the cult status their products have reached. In the case of the iPhone, the production cost is very low, leaving a profit to Apple of an astonishing USD 270 per device in some cases. Similarly, Emirates has achieved among the lowest operating costs in its industry yet at face value is seen to command comparatively high retail prices.

Brazilian cosmetics company Natura has also emerged with a fresh approach to mitigating costs. One example is its community-based sales organization which bears the hallmarks of a crowd-based strategy. Its sales and acquisition costs are as a result much lower than those of its peers, creating significantly above-average profitability.

Conversely, Nokia has anything but a lean cost structure. Running an expensive organization with by far the highest spending on R&D in the industry could only work in a market leader scenario without the presence of circling black swans. When the unimaginable happened, this unsustainable cost structure was Nokia's undoing.

The X-factor dimension is simply missing in the conventional paradigm. Nowhere in the cookbook recipes do we see any room left for a hidden ingredient: the unexplained. The procedures and analyses surrounding strategy processes are laid down in a rational fashion. In the emerging paradigm, the picture looks very different. Here, seemingly irrational strategic moves carry significance and are taken seriously. Moving into the unknown universe is precisely what the black swan aims to do, in order to discover and exploit a special competence or set of skills it can harness to maximum impact. Huawei's military strategy, Steve Jobs' return to Apple, Ryanair's harnessing of its CEO's aggressive, extrovert personality and willingness to court controversy, are all examples of this. Indeed, all of our black swan case studies exhibit these traits.

The regulatory dimension is only marginally addressed in the conventional paradigm, if at all. In the emerging paradigm its importance is becoming increasingly acknowledged across many industries. The airline, electricity, railways, telecommunications, banking, pharmaceuticals, postal, and other industries bear regulation as their single biggest uncertainty affecting demand, capital expenditure, and image. It can be equally important competitively, too—for example if a black swan is suddenly able to gain a regulatory advantage where others suffer disadvantages. Since future regulatory requirements are often the great unknown, this is a welcome environment for the adventurous, pioneering black swan that is happy to paddle into murkier waters.

Typically black swans have a firm hand on the regulatory dimension. Huawei receiving a helping hand from the Chinese government; Apple had no hesitation in suing its competitors for apparent regulatory breaches; Ryanair has deliberately courted serious regulatory conflict (gaining great media exposure in the process); Emirates has benefited substantially from favorably regulated airport facilities in its home market; and both of these airlines, with relatively new fleets of aircraft, have exploited this situation to their advantage, demanding that regulatory agencies impose stringent regulation on other carriers based on their CO_2 emissions.

Clearly, the regulatory dimension is a double-edged sword as some company activities may need regulatory approval in foreign geographies, and some governments may choose to support companies through industrial policies, export credits, governmental promotions, and similar means. As there is no such thing as uniform global regulation of companies, this places competitors on an uneven playing field. Regulatory approval and forbearance differ from country to country, as does each country's eagerness to support its own domestic companies. Amid all this chaos, in swoop the black swans, taking full advantage of this 'Wild West' environment.

This is yet another example of *Extremistan*, where companies resist conforming and where the modus operandi is to cultivate and thrive amid the unknowns.

RETURN ON STRATEGY

Until now black swan companies have been largely overlooked by strategy experts, despite their highly disruptive presence and their explosive impact on all that is accepted and comfortable. This exposes a major gap in current strategic theory thinking, prompting us to talk in terms of an *emerging* paradigm. There is an urgent need to bridge the gap between strategy theory and practice—not least because any company looking to succeed in its chosen field would be made not to want to replicate the successes of high-profile mavericks, or to protect its interests so that its own achievements are not undermined by an unwelcome incomer in the future.

Researchers like Taleb and Kahneman[7] address the fallacy around the way that flawed stories of the past can shape our views of the world today and predictions about the future. Our narratives of the past may make it difficult for us to accept that there are limits to our forecasting ability. In hindsight, everything may make sense and so that it seems to have been predictable yesterday. This in turn leads to overconfidence in our ability to predict the future.

The big question that remains is whether the black swans analyzed in this book will continue to thrive. The only credible answer to this is that we don't know! It is likely to depend on the extent to which each player continues to stay sharp and alert, honing its black swan qualities and refusing to change its colors.

Even within our examples of black swans there are differences, and perhaps this could have a bearing on how their respective stories play out. The differences are set out in Table 13.4.

Uniting all of them is the element of surprise; the ability to catch incumbents unawares. But the way they did this, or were able to do this, differs subtly.

When Tata Motors suddenly got the opportunity to acquire Jaguar Land Rover because of lack of interest from others; when Huawei happened to base all of

Table 13.4
Black Swan Types[8]

Type of black swan disruption		Black Swan Strategy	
		Intentionally	*Serendipitously*
	Maverick	Ryanair	Tata Motors
	Frugal	Aravind/Natura	Huawei
	Cross-boundary	Apple	Emirates

its products on the new IP technology; and when Emirates was able to take a chance on the back of poor-performing Gulfair and the simultaneous meteoric rise of Dubai, there was a considerable degree of serendipity attached. The actions of Ryanair, Aravind, Natura, and Apple were more intentional, albeit that each differed in the type of disruption pursued. In the case of Ryanair, CEO O'Leary pursued a maverick type of disruption, initially competing head on with British Airways. Aravind and Nature based their disruption to a large extent on frugality, including finding ways from the outset to do more for less in emerging economies. The same characterizes Huawei. In the case of Apple, the disruption was extensive and crossed boundaries, taking the company into markets no one could have expected—from telecoms to multimedia content.

But even from these further analyses we are not left with consistent indicators of success, so we are unable to extrapolate confidently, or perform onward predictions. Moreover, just because a black swan company has pursued one strategy and one type of disruption at a particular phase in its development, it does not automatically follow that it will continue in the same vein. Rather, it may wish to develop another type of strategy and disruption in a future phase.

Fortunately this book is not about predictions. Rather it examines and exposes some of the fallacies and shortcomings of rational strategic thinking, suggesting that companies might pursue an even higher Return on Strategy if they are able to look into the unknown universe. As we have shown, this means acknowledging and exploring:

- *The surprise dimension*—being alert to the opportunities to execute the unexpected (rather than always doing what outsiders expect).
- *The innovation dimension*—executing *next* practice passionately in revolutionary steps (rather than muddling through incrementally).
- *The cost dimension*—thinking in terms of disruption (rather than solely value creation)
- *The X-factor dimension*—exploiting a specific set of competencies in a manner which nobody expected (rather than just discounting the unknown).

■ *The regulatory dimension*—addressing the fact that a growing part of the competition is based on regulatory contingencies (rather than overlooking regulatory matters and focusing on pure market-based relationships).

Above all, this book calls for a new mindset around strategy—one where strategists do not disregard the unknown universe and the associated risks and uncertainty. The time has come to deal with ambiguity and the unplanned. We call this new way of thinking the *ambidextrous* mindset.

By this we mean the ability to think and act in a different and a radically new way, handling ambiguity and complexity in a value creating way for the organization. Instead of solely focusing on barriers the ambidextrous leader utilizes contingencies to develop new solutions may be in a disruptive way as could be seen in the case examples earlier discussed. The ambidextrous leader does not stick to 'either/or' solutions but demonstrate 'both/and' approaches. The ambidextrous leader is therefore capable of managing paradoxes and to release the potential embedded in the X factor.

Some might raise the question whether an ambidextrous mindset can be learned. Our observations and experiences indicate that some might have the ambidextrous DNA from birth. However, we are also convinced that personal training and practices can stretch this mode of behaving of many leaders. But it requires an awareness and consciousness about own performance style. Finding and attaining the right balance to achieve an ambidextrous mindset may be accomplished by funneling problems, conditions, ideas, and concepts through our right brains to our left brains. It might sound easy, but it requires the ability to tap into our most resourceful mechanism—the whole human brain. When combining both thought patterns of each hemisphere, leaders are accomplishing the ultimate in human behavior. Not only do they enable themselves to exhibit and maintain peak human analytical performance, they are also allowing themselves to receive their atmospheric conditions or situations with an open mind.

The more leaders and organizations can fertilize this type of behavior the stronger black swans can take off.

BEYOND STRATEGY

In terms of corporate business strategy, the first logical step is to examine the inner workings of black swan companies, because they are the foremost representative of this new mindset.

Companies with a business-as-usual approach, a lack of imagination, an unchanged mindset, and a blind adherence to the conventional paradigm face a rapidly growing challenge—one that is in most cases unknown to them. However, the risks attached to this incumbent positioning could also be converted to an opportunity.

The need to go *beyond strategy* may be relevant not only for present and future black swan companies, then, but also to incumbents—in order to remove present blind spots and develop new business opportunities.

The implications for future work that goes 'beyond strategy' are huge. New terminology might include:

■ Moving away from the *conventional paradigm* and taking a deeper look into the *emerging paradigm* while continuing to develop the latter.
■ Looking much more into the *ambidextrous agility* of companies so that the new toolbox can adequately address growing complexity, uncertainty, and globalization.
■ Better tools to distinguish between complacent attitudes and positioning, and real 'hunger for change'.[9]
■ An ability to look deeper into business models which are *disruptive by nature* or—when looking at incumbents—to assess the *fragility and anti-fragility* of these organizations.[10]

The toolkit presented in Appendices 1 and 2 may be the first step towards addressing a world that is becoming increasingly populated by black swans.

KEY REFLECTIONS

A. Black swans are often seen to achieve a disproportionately high Return on Strategy because they know how to exploit the unknown universe, catching conventional companies by surprise. Is it a fair observation that too little attention has been given to the understanding of the inner workings of black swans until now, and how they can contribute to the emerging new paradigm for business strategy?

B. Working with black swan companies could be a goldmine, building up knowledge about what would otherwise be left unknown—for the benefit of both would-be black swans *and* current incumbents. As long as they work exclusively with conventional strategy, companies and strategy experts will continue to be blind to their own blindness.

C. Managers with an ambidextrous mindset tend to follow a more unconventional strategy, enabling their companies to move towards a black swan mode.

D. In the day-to-day work with strategy we need to open up the toolkit, reject some of the existing equipment and develop some new tools in order to increase the Return on Strategy. Some of the tools to date can be found in this book, including its appendices.

NOTES

1 McGrath, Rita Gunther (2013), *The End of Competitive Advantage* (see also: http.//hbr. org/2013/06/transient-advantage).
2 See Rosenzweig, Phil (2007), *The Halo Effect*.
3 Our black swan window is somewhat inspired by the Johari Window, originally created by Joseph Luft and Harrington Ingham as far back as the 1950s, and used to help people better understand their relationship with self and others. It is used primarily in self-help groups and corporate settings as a heuristic exercise. See Luft, J. and Ingham, H. (1950), The Johari Window, a Graphic Model of Interpersonal Awareness, *Proceedings of the western training laboratory in group development* (Los Angeles, UCLA). However, we use this technique in the context of corporate strategy and essentially as a stepping stone to our own Figure 13.1 which we are working with using our own strategy consulting practice, see also Appendix 1, in particular when addressing the question on "how good will a company be at turning 'unknowns' into 'knowns.'"
4 See McGrath, Rita Gunther (2013), *The End of Competitive Advantage*.
5 Essentially, this quadrant deals with a scenario where the company's mindset is entering the subconscious sphere not seen/recognized by others.
6 See some of our examples in *Return on Strategy*, notably the case of Hotmail, which was neither developed knowingly by the founders, nor seen by external stakeholders in the early days (Andersen, Froholt, and Poulfelt (2010).
7 See Taleb, Nassim Nicholas (2010), *The Black Swan*, notably pp. 135ff.; Kahneman, Daniel (2011), *Thinking fast and slow*, notably pp. 199ff.
8 This typology is proprietarily composed but based on inspiration from an SMS Special Conference, Strategizing Practices from the Outliers: Enabling Big Bang Innovation, especially from different speeches by Professor Robert A. Burgelman, Stanford University, Liisa Välikangas, Aalto University, Professor Pasha Mahmood from IMD Lausanne, and Professor Julian Birkinshaw, London Business School.
9 The term 'hunger for change' is borrowed from an IBM CEO study (2008).
10 See Taleb, Nassim Nicholas (2012), *Antifragile*, Allen Lane, London.

Metrics and Diagnostics

There are many practical diagnostic routes which help companies become prepared at a higher level of consciousness. This appendix tries to provide some inroads showing how companies might progress their black swan efforts. As part of our consulting practice we have developed a series of tools to help companies address several of the issues highlighted in this book. Among these are three handy tools/metrics:

i. *How agile is the company?* This metric is to be able to address—at a general level and in a relatively rapid fashion—the strategic potential of the company in terms of its ability to move quickly. In the case of (potential) black swans this is important so that they are able to exploit the surprise dimension. In the case of incumbents, this tool/metric is also important—allowing them to assess how quickly and well they would be able to react to sudden market disruption by a black swan.

ii. *How good will a company be at recognizing and preparing themselves for 'unknowns'—i.e. events/developments/market shifts that haven't happened yet?* Arguably most companies operate only within certain parts of the 'known' universe. Yet many of the great opportunities (upsides) or severe risks (downsides) belong to the unknown universe. We offer a tool to help with this, but without metrics at this point because it is too early in the research journey to have enough statistical evidence to draw on.

iii. *Do you have a sufficient amount of points in order to potentially emerge as black swan?* This tool helps to establish the extent to which a company may be tainted/constrained by methods set out in the conventional paradigm; or conversely how well placed it is, or how well it might adapt to the emerging new paradigm.

Any metrics will need to be interpreted heuristically. Remember that even under the conventional paradigm a company may do well as a 'white swan' for a limited period of time. With modifications and reservations, the more a company is able and willing to take methodologies on board from the emerging paradigm, the better they are likely to fare over the long term in this dynamic world of constant change.

Even if they may be quite crude initiative, such metrics are useful in that they facilitate dialogue about strategy and allow us to test of the temperature of a company, before then 'going deep.'

1. HOW AGILE IS THE COMPANY? (INITIAL ASSESSMENT)

Focused on "as is"/ conventional	Scale	Ready for/Open to the emerging paradigm universe
We use a well-known concept	1 2 3 4 5	We emphasize experiments
Crafting a good well-documented strategic plan is key	1 2 3 4 5	Developing agility is key to meeting challenges
Our strategic plan fits well with our budgeting process	1 2 3 4 5	Strategy and budget are not correlated
We strive to get the best out of all our resources	1 2 3 4 5	We rely on a selected part of our resources
Analysis is more important than experiments	1 2 3 4 5	Experiments are more important than analysis
Our core competencies are more important than uncertain opportunities	1 2 3 4 5	We always look for new opportunities first
We prioritize developing sustained competitive advantage over time	1 2 3 4 5	We prioritize taking the market by surprise
It is important to avoid failures	1 2 3 4 5	A trial and error culture is important

Key:

  1 = Agree fully with the proposition to the left
  2 = Agree partially with the proposition to the left
  3 = I am somewhere in the middle
  4 = Agree partially with the proposition to the right
  5 = Agree fully with the proposition to the right

2. IDENTIFICATION OF THE LEVEL OF KNOWN AND UNKNOWNS: HOW GOOD WILL A COMPANY BE AT TURNING 'UNKNOWNS' INTO 'KNOWNS'

Of course it is very difficult to predict the unpredictable and turn unknowns into knowns. We have had the opportunity during strategy work to employ techniques based on heuristic methods.

The starting point is to pair your own mindset with what is externally recognized, as outlined in Chapter 13.

In order to further develop this generic tool, we can observe that the conventional paradigm covers part of quadrant 1 of Table A1.1—the known/known quadrant and, at best, a slice of what we have called the opportunity spot (i.e. the window of opportunity/what is known to *you* but what is unknown *externally*) (see Figure A1.1).

Table A1.1

		External Recognition			
		Known		**Unknown**	
Own Mindset	**Unknown**	Unknown/Known	2	3	Unknown/Unknown
	Known	Known/Known	1	4	Known/Unknown

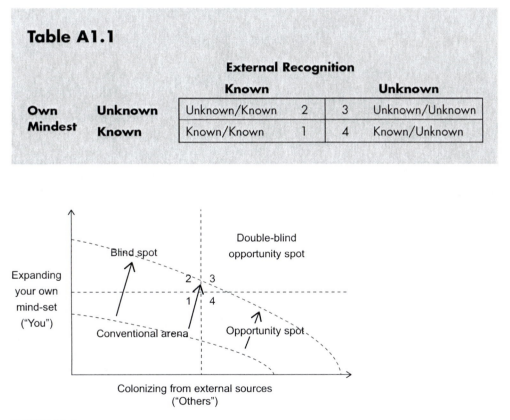

FIGURE A1.1

When trying to make unknowns more known, we work with the relative size of the four quadrants and use a combination of open questions and forced choice.

In order to delve deeper into quadrant 2, we ask the following types of question:

A. How much do you value engaging in commercial experimentation?
B. When you develop and test ideas, are we then talking about known concepts or something which has not yet been brought to the market by anyone?
C. How much does your strategic thinking rely on past experience?
D. Do you use best-practice methodology, i.e. look at existing industry practices and then benchmark yourself, or import best practice from another company? Or do you look for what could become 'next' or 'new' practices?
E. To what extent do you explore what you do not know about: (a) the market; (b) competitors; (c) trends in the industry; (d) cross-industry developments, etc.?
F. Do you actively seek feedback from external sources on industry matters?
G. If there are relevant things out there which are unknown to you but may be known by others, you are at risk of an ignorance which could undermine your success in the future. What do you consider to be your level of ignorance?
H. Do you work with analytics when monitoring your competitors, market trends, etc.?

This technique helps managers enlarge their known universe and make former blind spots visible. Each quadrant can be changed to reflect the relevant proportions of each type of knowledge internally ('you') as well as externally ('others') (see Figure A1.2).

Moving to quadrant 3 is actually more difficult, because it is what we label the 'double-blind opportunity spot.' With this in mind, we will first address quadrant 4 before reverting to quadrant 3.

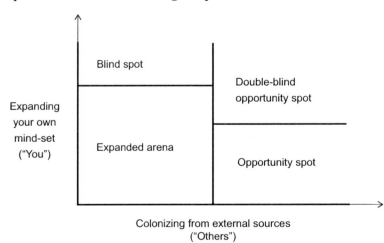

FIGURE A1.2

For quadrant 4 we would usually bring into play questions such as:

A. To what extent are you aware that you can catch the market by surprise?
B. Do you keep track of what you know but your peers do not know?
C. Will a competitor's so-called sustained competitive advantage be something which presents an opportunity for tactical moves from your side?
D. What are your tactics with regard to what you will expose, and when, about matters that are known to you but unknown to others?
E. How do you use analytics as part of a self-discovery exercise?

By probing at this level we hope to get companies on the road to expanding the arena, so that they can take advantage of the opportunity territory (see Figure A1.3).

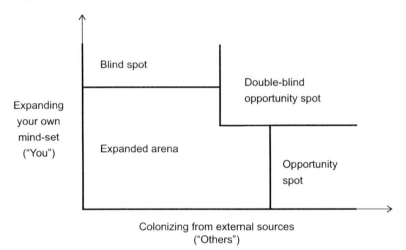

FIGURE A1.3

This brings us back to quadrant three, the so-called double blind opportunity spot. Although this is the most difficult quadrant to work with, we approach it by way of very simple questions, such as:

A. How do you develop talent?
B. What does the idea of an X factor mean to you and your organization?
C. Are Delphi-like techniques parts of your toolkit?
D. How do you utilize big data analytics in order to gain new knowledge and drive innovation?

See Figure A1.4 for expansion into quadrant 3.

We have covered the role of the X factor more comprehensively in our book, *Return on Strategy*, (Andersen et al., 2010) to which reference is made (see also www.returnonstrategy.org).

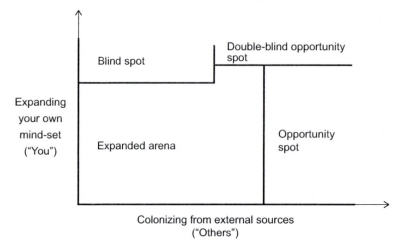

FIGURE A1.4

3. POINTS TO GAIN IN THE BLACK SWAN UNIVERSE: DO YOU SCORE HIGHLY ENOUGH/ HAVE YOU GOT WHAT IT TAKES TO EMERGE AS A BLACK SWAN?

A. The first black swan questionnaire addresses how the interviewee sees strategic status in the company 'as is'.

Today, Company X is characterized by taking the following strategic weapons into account:

Either	Scale	Or
Market leadership	**1 2 3 4 5**	*Zero market share = perfect start*
First mover, pole position, and sustainable advantages	**1 2 3 4 5**	*Late or last or unexpected mover and ephemeral advantages*
Differentiate and value creation	**1 2 3 4 5**	*Innovate substantially and impact tactics*
Marginal/incremental	**1 2 3 4 5**	*Revolutionary, unprecedented leaps*
Best practice	**1 2 3 4 5**	*Next practice*
Analytical	**1 2 3 4 5**	*Passionate*
Conventional cost structure	**1 2 3 4 5**	*Disruptive cost structure*
Analytical	**1 2 3 4 5**	*Passionate*
Everything explained/ planned	**1 2 3 4 5**	*Focus on exploitation of the X dimension (the unexplained, the unplanned, the unexpected)*

Market forces	**1 2 3 4 5**	Regulatory distortions/wins
Marginally or not addressed	**1 2 3 4 5**	Regulatory game-changing
Marginally or not addressed	**1 2 3 4 5**	National subsidies, home market, or cultural advantages

Key:

1 = Agree fully with the proposition to the left
2 = Agree partially with the proposition to the left
3 = I am somewhere in the middle
4 = Agree partially with the proposition to the right
5 = Agree fully with the proposition to the right

B. The second black swan questionnaire addresses how the interviewee sees the desired/ideal strategic status in the company.

Going forward, Company X should ideally be characterized by taking the following strategic weapons into account:

Either	Scale	Or
Market leadership	**1 2 3 4 5**	Zero market share = perfect start
First mover, pole position, and sustainable advantages	**1 2 3 4 5**	Late or last or unexpected mover and ephemeral advantages
Differentiate and value creation	**1 2 3 4 5**	Innovate substantially and impact tactics
Marginal/incremental	**1 2 3 4 5**	Revolutionary, unprecedented leaps
Best practice	**1 2 3 4 5**	Next practice
Analytical	**1 2 3 4 5**	Passionate
Conventional cost structure	**1 2 3 4 5**	Disruptive cost structure
Analytical	**1 2 3 4 5**	Passionate
Everything explained/ planned	**1 2 3 4 5**	Focus on exploitation of the X dimension (the unexplained, the unplanned, the unexpected)
Market forces	**1 2 3 4 5**	Regulatory distortions/wins
Marginally or not addressed	**1 2 3 4 5**	Regulatory game-changing
Marginally or not addressed	**1 2 3 4 5**	National subsidies, home market, or cultural advantages

Key:

1 = Agree fully with the proposition to the left
2 = Agree partially with the proposition to the left

3 = I am somewhere in the middle

4 = Agree partially with the proposition to the right

5 = Agree fully with the proposition to the right

C.   Calculating your metrics.

On the basis of the questionnaire displayed under A and B, we are now able to calculate the following:

  i. The absolute number of points related to the organization 'as is'.
 ii. Gaps between the factual 'as is' and the normative 'should be'.
iii. The absolute number of points of 'should be'.
 iv. i, ii, and iii measured against benchmarks.

Company of the Future Metric

COMPANY OF THE FUTURE

Various analyses have been undertaken to determine what characterizes the company of the future. Below are ten important characteristics (a consolidation of many analyses and future scenarios):

1. Hungry for change

The company of the future (CF) is capable of changing quickly and successfully. Instead of primarily responding to trends, it shapes and leads them. Market and industry shifts are a chance to move ahead of the competition.

2. Innovative beyond customers' imagination

CF surpasses the expectations of increasingly demanding customers. Deep collaborative relationships allow it to surprise customers with innovations that make both its customers and its own business more successful.

3. Sticking to a transient strategy

CF recognizes that strategy needs to be reshaped and reconfigured continuously in order to achieve competitive edge and to capitalize on the transient advantages.

4. Disruptive by nature

CF radically challenges its business model, disrupting the basis of competition. It shifts the value proposition, overturns traditional delivery approaches and, as soon as opportunities arise, reinvents itself and its entire industry.

5. Globally integrated

CF maximizes integration opportunities to take advantage of today's global economy. Its business is strategically designed to access the best capabilities, knowledge, and assets from wherever they reside in the world and apply them wherever required in the world.

6. Democratizing information

CF has information systems that equip and allow every employee to act in the interests of the entire company.

7. High-performance culture

CF is permeated by a truly performance-driven culture that stimulates the winning behavior in a way that balances long-term goals with short-term gains.

8. Communities of passion and commitment

CF has a way of management that facilitates the creation of communities of passion and commitment, and through this enables the employees to optimize their engagement, satisfaction, and loyalty.

9. Genuine, not just generous

CF goes beyond philanthropy and compliance and reflects genuine concern for society in all actions and decisions.

10. Continuously fuelling leadership

CF continuously retrains and refuels its managerial minds to avoid the pull from the past and to challenge and open the mindset going forward.

The key question to ask yourself and your management team with regard to your company is: To what degree are we a company of the future?

Evaluate your organization today using the scale below, from where 1 is lowest and 5 is highest.

	1	2	3	4	5
	Very low				Very high

1. Hungry for change
2. Innovative beyond customers' imagination
3. Sticking to a transient strategy
4. Disruptive by nature

5. Globally integrated
6. Democratizing information
7. High-performance culture
8. Communities of passion and commitment
9. Genuine, not just generous
10. Continuously fuelling leadership

Key:

1 = Very low
2 = Partly Low
3 = Medium
4 = Partly high
5 = Very high

The model measures the degree to which organizations look like 'companies of the future', thereby assessing their strategic maturity, as below:

Score:

10–19:   Major overhaul needed
20–29:   Room for improvement
30–39:   Sound platform for take-off
40–50:   Next practice to be outlined

Bibliography

Andersen, H.C. (1844), *The Ugly Duckling* (translation).

Andersen, M. Moesgaard and Poulfelt, F. (2006), *Discount Business Strategy: How the new market leaders are redefining business strategy,* Wiley, New York.

Andersen, M. Moesgaard, Froholdt, M., and Poulfelt, F. (2010), *Return on Strategy: How to achieve it!* Routledge, Abingdon, UK.

Anderson, Chris (2009), *Free: The future of a radical price,* Hyperion, London.

Barley, Steve (2010), Building an institutional field to corral a government, *Organization Studies,* 31(6), 777–805.

Chabris, Christopher and Simons, Daniel (2011), *The Invisible Gorilla and Other Ways Our Intuition Deceives Us,* HarperCollins, London.

Christensen, Clayton M. (1997), *The Innovator's Dilemma: When new technologies cause great firms to fail,* Harvard Business School Press, Boston.

Clausewitz, Carl von (1997 edition), *On War,* Wordsworth Edition, Herts., UK.

Collins, J. (2001), *Why Some Companies Make the Leap . . . And Others Don't: Good to great,* Harper Business, New York.

Collins, Jim. and Hansen, Morten T. (2011), *Great by Choice,* Harper Business, New York.

Collins, Jim. and Porras, Jerry (1994), *Built to Last: Successful habits of visionary companies,* Harper Business, New York.

Eccles, Serafeim, Heffernan (2012), *Natura Cosmeticos S.A.,* Harvard Business School case no. 9-412-052.

EIU (2008), *Global Disruptors: Steering through the storms* (London).

EIU (2011), *The Long View: Getting new perspective on strategic risk* (London).

Finkelstein, Sydney, Harvey, C., and Lawton, T. (2007), *Breakout Strategy: Meeting the challenge of double-digit growth,* McGraw-Hill, New York.

Foss and Lindenberg (2013). Microfoundations for Strategy: A goal-framing perspective on the drivers of value creation, *Academy of Management Perspectives,* 27(2), 85–102, in particular on an oblique approach and transformational leadership.

Friedman, Milton (1970), The social responsibility of business is to increase its profits, *New York Times Magazine,* September 13.

Fuentelsaz, L. et al. (2012), Production technologies and financial performance: The effect of uneven diffusion among competitors, *Research Policy.*

Gifford, Jonathan (2012), *Blindsided: How business and society are shaped by our irrational and unpredictable behavior.* Marshall Cavendish Business, London.

Govindarajan, Vijay and Trimble, Chris (October 2009), How GE is disrupting itself, *Harvard Business Review.*

Govindarajan, Vijay and Trimble, Chris (2012), *Reverse Innovation: Create far from home win everywhere,* Harvard Business Review Press, Boston.

Hamel, Gary (2012), *What Matters Now: How to win in a world of relentless change, ferocious competition, and unstoppable innovation,* Jossey-Bass, New York.

Haque, Umair (2011), *The New Capitalist Manifesto—Building a disruptively better business,* Harvard Business Review Press, Boston.

Hawkins, D.M. (1980), *Identification of Outliers,* Chapman, London.

IBM Global CEO Study (2008), *The Enterprise of the Future.*

Isaacson, Walter (2011), *Steve Jobs.* Simon & Schuster, New York.

Johnson et al. (2011), *Exploring Strategy,* 9th ed., FT Prentice Hall, Essex, UK.

Joyce, William, Nohria, Nitin, and Roberson, Bruce (2004), *What (Really) Works: The 4+2 formula for sustained business success,* Harper Business, New York.

Kahneman, Daniel (2011), *Thinking Fast and Slow,* Allen Lane, New York.

Kim, W. Chan and Mauborgne, R. (2005), *Blue Ocean Strategy: How to create uncontested market space and make the competition irrelevant,* Harvard Business School Press, Boston.

Lashinsky, Adam (2012), *Inside Apple,* John Murray, London.

Luft, J. and Ingham, H. (1950), The Johari Window, a Graphic Model of Interpersonal Awareness. *Proceedings of the western training laboratory in group development* (Los Angeles, UCLA).

Maier, Matthew (2005), Rise of the Emirates' Empire, *CNN Money,* October 1.

McGilchrist, Iain (2009), *The Master and His Emissary: The divided brain and the making of the Western World,* Yale University Press, New Haven, CT.

McGill, Michael (1988), *The American Business and the Quick Fix,* Henry Holt, New York.

McGrath, Rita Gunther (2013), *The End of Competitive Advantage: How to keep your strategy moving as fast as your business,* Harvard Business Review Press, Boston.

Mintzberg, Henry (2005), *Managers Not MBAs: A hard look at the soft practice of managing and management development.* Berrett-Koehler Publishers, San Francisco.

Mullings, John and Komisar, Randy (2009), *Getting to Plan B: Breaking through to a better business model,* Harvard Business Press, Boston.

Palley, Thomas (2008), *Breaking the Neoclassical Monopoly in Economics* (Project-syndicate.org, January 31).

Paukku, Markus and Välikangas, Liisa (2012), Outlier Organizations and Systematic Transitions: Towards a research agenda, *Strategic Management Society,* 31st Conference, Prague, September.

Peters, T.J. and Waterman, R.H. (1982), *In Search of Excellence: Lessons from America's Best-Run Companies,* Harper & Row, New York.

Pink, Daniel (2010), *Drive: The Surprising Truth About What Motivates Us,* Canongate, London.

Porter, M.E. (1980), *Competitive Advantage: Creating and sustaining superior performance,* Free Press, New York.

Porter, Michael (1980), *Competitive Strategy,* Free Press, New York.

Porter, Michael (1985), *Competitive Advantage,* Free Press, New York.

Porter, Michael (2008), The five competitive forces that shape strategy, *Harvard Business Review.*

Prahalad, C.K. and Hamel, Gary (1994), *Competing for the Future,* Harvard Business School Press, Boston.

Pratt, Michael G. (2000), The good, the bad, and the ambivalent: Managing identification among Amway distributors, *Administrative Science Quarterly,* 45, 456–493.

Roger, Martin (July 2010), The execution trap, *Harvard Business Review.*

Rope, S. et al. (2008), Modelling the innovation value chain, *Research Policy,* 37(6–7), 961–977.

Rosenzweig, Phil (2007), *The Halo Effect: . . . And the eight other business delusions that deceive managers,* Free Press, New York.

Rumelt, Richard (2012), *Good Strategy Bad Strategy: The difference and why it matters*, Profile Books, London.

Schumpeter, Joseph (1942), *Capitalism, Socialism and Democracy*, Harper & Row, New York.

Sheth, Jagdish (2007), *The Self-Destructive Habits of Good Companies*, Wharton School Publishing, Upper Saddle River, NJ.

Smith, Adam (1976), *The Wealth of Nations*, edited by R.H. Campbell and A.S. Skinner, Glasgow edition of the Works and Correspondence of Adam Smith

Stigler, George J. (1971), The theory of economic regulation, *Bell Journal of Economics and Management Science*, 2(1), 3–21.

Stout, Lynn A. (June 2012), The problem of corporate purpose, *Issues in Governance Studies* (48).

Sull, Donald N., Ghoshal, Sumantra, and Monteiro, Felipe (Spring 2005), The Hub of the world, *Business Strategy Review*.

Taleb, Nassim Nicholas (2010), *The Black Swan: The impact of the highly improbable*, Random House, New York.

Taleb, Nassim Nicholas (2012), *Antifragile*, Allen Lane, London.

Tjan, Anthony K., Harrington, Richard J., and Hsieh, Tsun Yan (2012), *Heart, Smarts, Guts, and Luck*, Harvard Business Review Press, Boston.

Index

Note: 'N' after a page number indicates a note; 'f' indicates a figure; 't' indicates a table.